# AMERICAN ZION

## QUANTIFYING JEWISH INFLUENCE IN THE UNITED STATES

SHAWN RYAN ROSA

ISBN: 1495453944

ISBN 13: 9781495453946

Library of Congress Control Number: 2014902881
CreateSpace Independent Publishing Platform
North Charleston, South Carolina

"TO LEARN WHO RULES
OVER YOU, SIMPLY FIND
OUT WHO YOU ARE NOT
ALLOWED TO CRITICIZE"

— VOLTAIRE

# TABLE OF CONTENTS

# INTRODUCTION

Do Jews really control the workings of the United States of America? This provocative question has been posed innumerable times, but the topic has not been discussed at length because certain quarters have effectively closed it off from discussion. These days, to merely ask this question is to be instantly labeled anti-Semitic. To write an entire book on the subject is to risk irrevocable excommunication from society itself.

The issue of Jewish power and influence in America presents itself, or rather leaps out, when the most casual of observers notices how many Jews occupy important positions within our society. Of course, America's Jews do not control *everything* (if only because they lack the raw numbers). However, it is indisputably true that Jews occupy a number of positions of power and influence that greatly outdistances their percentage of the overall population. In fact, based on the number of important positions they hold, one would think Jewish-Americans comprise, at the very least, a majority of the population in 2014.

Jews are firmly entrenched as the leaders of the most important segments of our society, able to control what the masses hear, read, and watch. Whether intentional or not, Jews have this amazing level of power in the United States because they occupy the positions which control these exact actions. He who runs a radio station can control what people hear. He who runs a newspaper can control what people read. And he who runs a television network can control what people watch.

This, however, is not to allege a conspiracy of any type. Merely stating that Jews control the most important segments of American society is not the same as saying that Jews secretly band together in order to assert their dominance over the roughly three hundred million Gentiles that comprise the vast majority of the population. Within these pages, you will not hear conspiracy theories relating to Jewish control in America. You will not hear about the "Protocols of the Learned Elders of Zion," the "Blood Libel," or any other myths that seek to paint Jewish people in a negative light. In fact, the manner in which Jews have come to obtain such unprecedented power in America is not even an issue covered herein. The purpose of this work, rather, is to quantify Jewish power in America as of 2014 and, to a lesser extent, explain the consequences of that power.

There number of important individual positions in the United States is more or less finite. The people occupying those positions are either Jewish or they are not, simple as that. However, those individuals can use the power they wield as they wish and it is possible to discern just how that power is being employed. America's Jews are concentrated in a handful of geographical locations, they generally come from similar socio-economic backgrounds, and their insular community generally supports a shared world view. As such, and contrary to what some scholars believe, important Jews in America can and do use their power to promote common goals. Again, this is not to allege a conspiracy. Just as Jews do not collaborate amongst themselves in an effort to wrest control of the United States away from non-Jews, those Jews already occupying positions of power do not secretly join forces and decide how to direct American affairs. The fact remains, though, that people from similar origins are often like-minded. Therefore, powerful

Jewish-Americans often support similar causes - not always, but quite often.

It is worth reiterating that, as discussed in my previous book, *On the Precipice: Constructing a Strategic Plan to Save the American Empire from Extinction,* honest inquiry into this issue has been closed off by the liberal media and the Jewish lobby.[1] And to attempt to re-open the issue for debate is to be instantly labeled anti-Semitic. Regardless, we must, as a nation, carefully consider Jewish power in America no matter what the cost. If it can be proven that Jewish influence in America is far greater than it should be, and if it can be further proven that Jewish influence in America has an overall negative impact on the country itself, then all the labeling and name-calling in the world will only illustrate that certain segments of the population have absolutely no interest in free and unbounded debate. For the easiest thing to do in relation to this issue is to label an individual anti-Semitic because their opinion is substantive and truthful. As we shall see in a later section, the deplorable reality is that is has become routine for those in positions of power in America to baselessly smear as anti-Semitic anyone with the courage to question the current state of affairs.

There are nine segments into which the study of Jewish power in America can be divided: government, law, academia, the media, big business, real estate, entertainment, culture, and sports. And it can be definitely proven that Jews occupy an unjustifiable percentage of the positions of power in each of these areas, far more so than one would expect from a group of people so terribly limited in number. For the average American, this is crucially important because these are the critical areas that determine the manner in which we live our lives on a daily basis.

In and of itself, having a small cadre of Jews in control of these major segments of society is not necessarily a bad thing, which is to say that Jews are no better or worse than any other sub-sect of the population. The real issue is having such a small group of people, with its own inherent prejudices, controlling the manner in which such a large group of people exist.

I have taken the time to research and investigate the individuals and organizations that are most prominent in the nine aforementioned fields. In government, for example, I have researched the backgrounds of office holders in all three branches: executive, legislative, and judicial. In the media I have personally researched the backgrounds of the individuals that own America's foremost newspapers and magazines. And in academia I have investigated the administrators and professors of all eight Ivy League institutions. It is not hyperbole to state that the resulting list of American power-holders reads like the membership of a Jewish Community Center.

To be sure, determining whether an important public figure is Jewish is not always as easy as it may seem. Spotting Jewish surnames, for instance, is not foolproof. Not only are there powerful Gentiles with Jewish-sounding surnames, but there are also influential women with Jewish surnames acquired solely through marriage. As such, I have chosen to exclude from this work the names of those individuals about whose Jewish background I am not highly certain. Accordingly, this analysis of Jewish power in the United States should be considered conservative in nature. This notation shall also explain why the reader will witness, in certain sections, phrases such as, "no less than one hundred thirty members of the 2012 *Forbes 400* are Jewish." That being said, it is probable that there are still likely to be several individuals included in this work that are not, in all honesty, Jewish. I apologize for this fact, but that is the nature of such a work as this, especially when then researcher does not have direct access to each and every individual involved. On the other hand, compiling this list in the conservative manner of which I have spoken also means that, if anything, I will likely be underestimating Jewish influence in America.

In addition to not including in this listing likely Jews whose backgrounds I was not highly certain of, I have also chosen to exclude from consideration individuals not meeting certain other requirements. First and foremost, deceased individuals are nearly entirely excluded from this study. Second, in proving Jewish influence in America it is preferable to include individuals still active in the affairs of the country. As such, this study is confined to Jews exerting influence in the United States since the late 1960s or early 1970s with a few important exceptions. To include for consideration Jews holding positions of power any earlier than this rough timeframe is to delve too far back into the nation's history to prove a point.

Once the goal of proving excessive Jewish influence in America has been accomplished we can then move to illustrating the common agenda that most powerful Jews in this country support, which is liberal and pro-Israel in nature. Again, this is not meant to insinuate a Jewish conspiracy in any manner. As stated earlier, powerful Jews are not in cahoots and do not gather together in secret meetings to form a liberal, pro-Israel union. Rather, such common interests naturally arise from a shared background and heritage. Furthermore, not every powerful Jew in the United States is necessarily interested in liberalism or supporting Israel. This is, however, the general agenda of a great many American Jews. To deny this fact is to be either naïve or disingenuous – voting records support the former claim, while the power of the Jewish Lobby in the United States supports the latter. Following the introduction to the specific agenda of the majority of powerful Jewish-Americans, examples will be given of the manner in which Jews attempt to persuade other Americans to support the causes they favor, as well as a brief recounting of the mistreatment of the few vocal opponents that have dared to confront their power and influence.

Before beginning our discussion in earnest, it is worthwhile to make note of a few stylistic issues that arise when writing on subject matter of such a sensitive nature as Jewish influence in America.

First, the word "Jew" has itself become a pejorative term in the United States thanks to the malignant effects of political correctness. There is, however, absolutely nothing wrong with using the word "Jew" in its written or spoken form. For centuries, the word "Jew" was a commonly accepted part of the English language - only in recent years has it come to be deemed politically incorrect. As an ardent opponent of political correctness, I will therefore continue to employ the word "Jew" throughout the course of this work. Second, it has become taboo to use certain phrases when writing or speaking about Jewish influence in America. The average person is now afraid to employ such words as "agenda" or "control" in reference to Jewish power because it seemingly connotes or infers a secret Jewish plan to assume power over other groups of people. Again, the recently banned usage of words like these in relation to Jews in America is merely a product of political correctness. Accordingly, I will not, under fear of being labeled anti-Semitic, refrain from using these and other similar words throughout the course of this book. I have already denounced Jewish conspiracy theories as slanderous falsehoods. There is, therefore, no legitimate reason to exclude such words from being used herein. Having noted several concerns that arise whenever an individual has the courage to question Jewish influence in the United States, we can now proceed with our investigation, beginning with a demographic profile of Jewish-Americans.

# JEWISH DEMOGRAPHICS

According to the 2010 census, the total population of the United States of America is 308 million, of which approximately 6.5 million are Jews.[2] Therefore, a mere two percent of the American population is Jewish.[3] There are not many Jews in the entire world. According to one estimate, the world's Jewish population is approximately 14 million.[4] According to its 2008 census, there are actually fewer Jews living in Israel, 5.6 million, than in the United States.[5] Almost the entire remainder of the world's Jewish population is scattered across Europe.

Research shows, however, that many people believe the percentage of the American population with Jewish heritage to be much greater than a mere two percent. Polls inquiring into what the average American believes the Jewish component of the population to be have resulted in figures of up to eighteen percent.[6] While many Americans are merely uninformed, it is safe to say that such a drastic difference between perception and reality owes itself mostly to the presence of so many Jews in positions of power. The average American, for example, is well aware that thousands of famous actors and musicians are Jewish. It logically follows that any individual would figure that America must be home to many Jews for so many of them to achieve such fame.

Nonetheless, only two percent of America's total population is Jewish. And the stability of that figure is a source of much concern for American Jews because while their numbers are not definitively shrinking, they are certainly not rising. In fact, no other subdivision of the American population is as concerned with preserving its own ranks as are Jews. One of the most oft-discussed topics in Jewish-American life is the issue of inter-faith marriage. This is the great paradox of Jewish liberalism. While Jews profess to be the most inclusive of America's various peoples, routinely espousing notions of love and friendship among races and religions, no other group has made preserving its own identity of such paramount importance.

Not surprisingly, Jews in America are clustered among themselves in only a handful of geographic locations. Of course, Jews are not unique among ethno-religious groups in this regard. Many of America's distinct peoples, sharing similar backgrounds, huddle together out of both necessity and preference. Still, America's Jews are collected in only a handful of places, most of which are centers of economic and political power.[7] Unsurprisingly, the state of New York is home to the single-highest number of Jews, 1.64 million, with the vast majority residing in New York City.[8] California, the only other state home to more than one million Jews, and home to Hollywood, has a Jewish population of 1.2 million.[9] Taken together, New York and California, combining for so many votes in the Electoral College, contain well over forty percent of the country's entire Jewish population. Florida, seemingly the primary destination for Jewish retirees, and New Jersey, more or less a suburb of New York City, are the only other states with more than five hundred thousand Jewish residents.[10] Simple math, then, tells us that sixty percent of all Jews, an overwhelming majority, live in one of only four different states.

But what more can we tell about America's Jewish population? Fortunately, excellent research has been conducted into the demographics of all of the country's ethno-religious groups. And while it is possible for a certain segment of people to live in close proximity to one another yet exhibit clear differences as individuals, it is safe to say that this is not the case among Jews. According to the Pew Forum on Religion & Public Life, America's Jewish population is far more homogenous than the country's Catholic, Evangelical Protestant, or Mainline Protestant populations.[11] Clearly, this is partially explained by the fact that these non-Jewish groups are much larger in size, which allows for greater diversity in many regards. However, factors such as exclusivity and a fiercely guarded mindset are what are truly responsible for the Jewish community's homogeneity, a topic that will be discussed in greater detail at a later point.

To begin with, the racial composition of America's Jewish community is ninety-five percent white. Only three percent of America's Jews characterize themselves as Hispanic and just two percent characterize themselves as black/mixed race.[12] Among Mainline Protestants (WASP), a lesser ninety-one percent of adherents characterize themselves as white. Among Evangelical Protestants, fifty percent of whom reside in the South, the percentage of white followers falls to eighty-one percent. Finally, the Catholic Church in America is the most diverse from a racial standpoint. While still a vast majority, only sixty-five percent of Catholics are white (nearly thirty percent of American Catholics are Hispanic).[13] As these figures indicate, if a person is not white then it is highly unlikely, nearly impossible, that such a person will identity as Jewish.

Of course, it will come as no surprise to many observes that nearly all Jews in America are white in terms of racial background. What the Pew Center has uncovered in terms of other facets of Jewish life is far more intriguing. Take, for instance, family life. While marital status among Jews (percentage of individuals married or never married) is nearly identical to that of Mainline Protestants, Evangelical Protestants, and Catholics, Jews actually have the lowest rate of divorce among these groups, even if only by a small amount.[14] This is surprising given the extent to which Jewish men in American entertainment go to illustrate how prickly Jewish wives can be. The stereotype of the "Jewish American Princess (JAP)," while obviously not always true, has arisen as a result of this type of humor.

Furthermore, the Pew Center has released findings about the average number of children that members of these four religious sects have residing in their respective homes. Seventy-two percent of Jewish households report having no children living with them, which compares to seventy percent for Mainline Protestants, sixty-five percent for Evangelical Protestants, and just sixty-one percent for Catholics.[15] While definitive conclusions about the implications of these figures are difficult to render, it may be that Jewish households expect their children to move out on their own and fend for themselves at a younger age.

The Pew Center has also revealed that Jewish-Americans cannot be equaled when it comes to educational achievement and personal income, which turns the question of Jewish power in the United States into a chicken-or-egg debate: do Jews control so many positions of power in America because they are highly educated or are Jews highly educated because they control so many positions of power (which are accompanied by levels of income that afford an elite education)? Answering such a complicated question does not fall within the purview of this work. However, illustrating demographic trends among America's Jews certainly does.

An impressive thirty-five percent of American Jews have reached the post-graduate level of college education. This figure compares more than favorably with just fourteen percent of Mainline Protests reaching the same level of education, just ten percent of Catholics reaching the same level of education, and just seven percent of Evangelical Protestants reaching the same level of education.[16] Regardless of the reasons behind these statistics, Jews are being educated at a higher rate than any other major group of Americans.

Income usually correlates directly to education and Jews in America, therefore, earn money more prolifically than other groups. Pew Center reports that an astounding forty-six percent of Jewish-Americans earn an annual income greater than $100,000. This figure is more than two times higher than that of Mainline Protestants, of whom only twenty-one percent earn six-figure salaries. Even more striking, only nineteen percent of Catholics and thirteen percent of Evangelical Protestants earn $100,000 on an annual basis.[17] Needless to say, ranking first among these groups in educational achievement and income allows America's Jews to exert an unparalleled level of control in the United States.

As stated earlier, it is actually a shared mindset and view of world affairs that binds America's Jews together, not the Jewish religion itself. Studies show that while Jews rank first in all of the foregoing categories, they are actually the least religious of the groups under consideration. Seventy-nine percent of Evangelical Protestants, fifty-six percent of Catholics, and fifty-two percent of Mainline Protestants state that religion is a "very important" part of their life, yet a mere thirty-one percent of Jews feel the same way.[18] This is not surprising as, by and large, American Jews, except for those of the Orthodox or Hasidic sub-sects of Judaism, are not known as being ultra-religious. It is also important to note that anti-Semitism, in the various forms it has taken within the United States, and worldwide, has never truly been founded upon a dislike for Jewish religious practice, but rather the perceived non-secular power and influence that Jews command.

Finally, numerous polls concerning the political leanings of America's Jewish contingent have indicated strong and readily observable patterns that apply to the vast majority of the Jewish community. This topic will be covered in greater depth at a later time, but for now it can be definitively stated that Jews in the United States are nearly entirely liberal in nature and highly Zionist in their outlook toward Israel. With a basic understanding of Jewish-American demographics now in hand, we may proceed to analyzing Jewish influence in nine of the most important segments of American life.

# JEWS IN GOVERNMENT

Of the nine areas that will be analyzed in this work, government exacts the greatest level of influence on the daily life of the average American. For it is government that sets the laws by which members of our society agree to live, it is government that determines how the money we contribute to the federal system as taxpayers will be spent, and it is government that determines the manner in which the United States interacts with the outside world. Elected or appointed, the individuals that occupy positions of power within the various branches of our government have a tremendous ability to determine the manner in which our lives unfold. And when so many of these power-holders originate from such a small portion of the population as that of America's Jewry, with its inherent prejudices, the result is that the preferences of two percent can be forced upon the remaining ninety-eight percent.

We will now begin quantifying Jewish power and influence in America by illustrating just how much Jewish-Americans are overrepresented in our government, from the federal level down to the governments of the largest American cities, as well as in organizations and bodies that, while not technically part of our government, exert considerable influence within the United States.

### *Federal Government*

<u>Executive Branch</u> - While the United States now has its first black president, it has yet to have a Jewish president or even a Jewish vice-president. However, the Jewish community has made up for not having a commander-in-chief from its own stock by entirely saturating the executive branch of the federal government; Jews have made themselves entirely at home in the West Wing of the White House.

*Office of the President* – The Office of the President includes such positions as chief of staff, national security advisor, White House counsel, senior advisor to the president, and the president's chief speech writers. The men and women that fill these crucially important positions have direct access to the president on a routine basis and can therefore influence policy decisions in a profound manner.

*–Chief of Staff* - In recent history, **no less than three of the past six chiefs of staff to the president, or fifty percent, have been Jewish** and include:

- Jacob Lew – Former chief of staff to Barack Obama
- Rahm Emanuel – Former chief of staff to Barack Obama
- Joshua Bolten – Former chief of staff to George W. Bush

*–National Security Advisor* – In recent history, **no less than two of the past six national security advisors, or thirty-three percent, have been Jewish** and include:

- Sandy Berger – Former national security advisor to Bill Clinton
- W. Anthony Lake – Former national security advisor to Bill Clinton

*–White House Counsel –* In recent history, **no less than four of the past twenty-one White House counsels, or nineteen percent, have been Jewish** and include:

- Robert Bauer – Former White House counsel under Barack Obama
- Bernard Nussbaum – Former White House counsel under Bill Clinton
- Robert Lipshutz – Former White House counsel under Jimmy Carter
- Leonard Garment – Former White House counsel under Richard Nixon

*–Senior Advisor to the President –* **Two of the past three senior advisors to the president, or sixty-seven percent, have been Jewish** and include:

- Valerie Jarrett – Current senior advisor to Barack Obama
- David Axelrod – Former senior advisor to Barack Obama

*–Chief Speech Writer –* From Richard Nixon to Barack Obama, **several Jews have served as chief speech writer for American presidents** and they include:

- Marc Thiessen – Former chief speech writer for George W. Bush
- David Frum – Former chief speech writer for George W. Bush
- Michael Waldman – Former chief speech writer for Bill Clinton
- Ben Stein – Former chief speech writer for Richard Nixon
- William Safire – Former chief speech writer for Richard Nixon

*Office of Management and Budget* – "The Office of Management and Budget assists the president in preparing his annual fiscal budget."[19] **The Office of Management and Budget is headed by a director, of which no less than five of the past eleven, or forty-five percent, have been Jewish** and include:

- Jeffrey Zients – Former director of the OMB under Barack Obama
- Jacob Lew – Former director of the OMB under Barack Obama
- Peter Orszag – Former director of the OMB under Barack Obama
- Joshua Bolten – Former director of the OMB under George W. Bush
- Alice Rivlin – Former director of the OMB under Bill Clinton

*Council of Economic Advisers* – The president consults with the Council of Economic Advisors on various fiscal matters. **The Council of Economic Advisors is headed by a chairman, of which no less than eleven of the past twenty, or fifty-five percent, have been Jewish** and include:

- Jay Furman – Current chairman of the CEA under Barack Obama
- Alan Krueger – Former chairman of the CEA under Barack Obama
- Edward Lazear – Former chairman of the CEA under George W. Bush
- Ben Bernanke - Former chairman of the CEA under George W. Bush
- Harvey Rosen – Former chairman of the CEA under George W. Bush
- Janet Yellen – Former chairman of the CEA under Bill Clinton

- Joseph Stiglitz – Former chairman of the CEA under Bill Clinton
- Michael Boskin – Former chairman of the CEA under George H.W. Bush
- Murray Weidenbaum – Former chairman of the CEA under Ronald Reagan
- Alan Greenspan – Former chairman of the CEA under Gerald Ford
- Herbert Stein – Former chairman of the CEA under Richard Nixon

*National Economic Council* – **The National Economic Council provides economic policy advice to the president and is headed by a director, of which no less than five of the past nine, or fifty-six percent, have been Jewish** and include:

- Jeffrey Zients – Current director of the NEA under Barack Obama
- Gene Sperling – Former director of the NEA under Barack Obama
- Lawrence Summers – Former director of the NEA under Barack Obama
- Stephen Friedman – Former director of the NEA under George W. Bush
- Robert Rubin – Former director of the NEA under Bill Clinton

*World Bank & International Monetary Fund* – Though the World Bank and the IMF are international institutions that do not operate under the jurisdiction of the United States government, it is nonetheless worthwhile to note their composition as they both work closely with the U.S. Treasury, the Federal Reserve, and the Securities and Exchange Commission. **The World Bank has had just twelve presidents since its founding in 1946, yet no less than five of them, or forty-two percent, have been Jewish** and include:

- Paul Wolfowitz – Former president of the World Bank
- James Wolfensohn – Former president of the World Bank
- Barber Conable – Former president of the World Bank
- Eugene Robert Black – Former president of the World Bank
- Eugene Meyer – Former president of the World Bank

**Dominique Strauss-Kahn, who is a French Jew, served as director of the International Monetary Fund until 2011**, at which time he was forced to resign the position in light of the sexual assault allegations that made him a household name in the United States.

*Office of the Vice President* – The Office of the Vice President includes all of the individuals that work to assist the vice president of the United States in conducting his daily responsibilities. **The vice president has his own chief of staff, of which no less than four of the past eight, or fifty percent, have been Jewish** and include:

- Ronald Klain – Former chief of staff to Joe Biden
- Lewis Libby – Former chief of staff to Dick Cheney
- Charles Burson – Former chief of staff to Al Gore
- William Kristol – Former chief of staff to Dan Quayle

Within the executive branch of the federal government there are fifteen major departments that report directly to the president of the United States. The heads of these fifteen departments form the president's cabinet. Among these fifteen departments, the Department of Defense, Department of State, Department of Justice, and Department of the Treasury are considered to be the most important. Jewish-Americans have come to exert an astounding level of power inside these four departments, which influence the daily lives of the American people in a profound manner.

*Department of Defense* – "The mission of the Department of Defense is to deter war and to protect the security of our country."[20] The Department of Defense is not only the largest government agency, but also the largest employer in the entire world with over three million people under its command.[21] The budget of the Department of Defense has soared to over $550 billion annually, a figure which represents far more than half of the entire discretionary spending of the United States.[22] **No less than four of the past thirteen secretaries of defense, or thirty-one percent, have been Jewish** and include:

- William Cohen – Former secretary of defense under Bill Clinton
- Caspar Weinberger – Former secretary of defense under Ronald Reagan
- Harold Brown – Former secretary of defense under Jimmy Carter
- James Schlesinger – Former secretary of defense under Richard Nixon

Other important figures in the Department of Defense include:

- Chuck Hagel – Current secretary of defense under Barack Obama – Hagel, who is not Jewish, was the first secretary of state to ever have his nomination for the position filibustered in the Senate because of his willingness to question Jewish influence in the United States
- Paul Wolfowitz – Former deputy secretary of defense under George W. Bush – Wolfowitz, who is Jewish, was the most influential deputy secretary of defense in the history of the United States

*Department of State* – "Plays the lead role in developing and implementing the president's foreign policy."[23] The Department of State employs approximately thirty thousand people, has an annual budget of roughly $35 billion, and is headed by the secretary of state.[24] **No less than two of the past thirteen secretaries of state, or fifteen percent, have been Jewish** and include:

- Madeleine Albright – Former secretary of state under Bill Clinton
- Henry Kissinger – Former secretary of state under Richard Nixon

*Department of Justice* – "The mission of the Department of Justice is to enforce the law and defend the interests of the United States according to the law."[25] The Department of Justice employs well over one hundred thousand people, has an annual budget of roughly $27 billion, and is headed by the attorney general.[26] **No less than two of the past twelve attorneys general, or seventeen percent, have been Jewish** and include:

- Michael Mukasey – Former attorney general under George W. Bush
- Edward Levi – Former attorney general under Gerald Ford

*Department of the Treasury* – "The Department of the Treasury is responsible for promoting economic prosperity and ensuring the soundness and security of the U.S. and international financial systems."[27] The Department of the Treasury employs over one hundred thousand people, has an annual budget of approximately $14 billion, and is headed by the secretary of the treasury.[28] **No less than five of the past seven secretaries of the treasury, or seventy-one percent, have been Jewish** and include:

- Jacob Lew – Current secretary of the treasury under Barack Obama
- Timothy Geitner – Former secretary of the treasury under Barack Obama
- Lawrence Summers – Former secretary of the treasury under Bill Clinton
- Robert Rubin - Former secretary of the treasury under Bill Clinton

- W. Michael Blumenthal – Former secretary of the treasury under Jimmy Carter

*Federal Reserve* – Serves as the central bank of the United States and establishes monetary policy. The Federal Reserve is overseen by a board of governors, the leader of which is known as the chairperson of the Federal Reserve. **No less than four of the past six chairs of the Federal Reserve, or sixty-seven percent, have been Jewish** and include:

- Janet Yellen – Current chairwoman of the Federal Reserve under Barack Obama
- Ben Bernanke – Former chairman of the Federal Reserve under Barack Obama
- Alan Greenspan – Former chairman of the Federal Reserve under George H.W. Bush
- Arthur F. Burns - Former chairman of the Federal Reserve under Richard Nixon

*Federal Deposit Insurance Corporation* – The FDIC is an independent agency operating under the auspices of the federal government, which insures the money deposited by private citizens into America's thousands of commercial banks. The FDIC was created in response to the bank runs witnessed during the Great Depression. **The current chairman of the FDIC under Barack Obama, Martin Gruenberg, is Jewish.**

*Securities and Exchange Commission* – "Holds primary responsibility for enforcing the federal securities laws and regulating the securities industry, the nation's stock and options exchanges, and other electronic securities markets in the United States."[29] **The Securities and Exchange Commission is headed by a chairperson, of which no less than two of the past three, or sixty-seven percent, have been Jewish** and include:

- Elisse Walter – Former chairperson of the SEC under Barack Obama
- Mary Schapiro – Former chairperson of the SEC under Barack Obama

Legislative Branch – With the Senate and the House of Representatives being composed of hundreds of individuals and changing in composition so frequently, it is beyond the scope of this book to chronicle Jewish influence in those two legislative bodies throughout even their more recent histories. However, we can analyze their current incarnations and observe the over-representation of Jews in both chambers of Congress. In particular, it worthwhile to note how many Jewish members of Congress hold leadership positions, which multiples their overall level of power.

*Senate* – **No less than eleven current senators are Jewish, of which ten are Democrats and one is an Independent. These twelve individuals represent a Senate that is therefore eleven percent Jewish**:

–Democrats:

- Michael Bennett – Colorado
- Richard Blumenthal – Connecticut
- Barbara Boxer – California, chairwoman of the Environment and Public Works Committee, chairwoman of the Select Committee on Ethics
- Ben Cardin – Maryland
- Diane Feinstein – California, chairwoman of the Select Committee on Intelligence
- Al Franken – Minnesota
- Carl Levin – Michigan, chairman of the Committee on Armed Services
- Brian Schatz – Hawaii

- Chuck Schumer – New York, chairman of the Democratic Policy and Communications Center, chairman of the Committee on Rules and Administration
- Ron Wyden - Oregon

–Independent:

- Bernie Saunders – Vermont (caucuses with the Democrats)

Note that three of the four senators representing the two most important states in the Union, California and New York, are Jewish – this despite the fact the Jews comprise a mere 3.3 percent of California's population and just 8.4 percent of New York's population.[30]

*House of Representatives* – **No less than twenty-two current representatives are Jewish, of which twenty-one are Democrats and just one a Republican. These twenty-two individuals represent a House of Representatives that is therefore five percent Jewish**:

–Democrats:

- David Cicilline – Rhode Island
- Stephen Cohen – Tennessee
- Susan Davis - California
- Theodore Deutch - Florida
- Elliot Engel – New York
- Lois Frankel - Florida
- Alan Grayson - Florida
- Steve Israel - New York, chairman of the Democratic Congressional Campaign Committee
- Sander Levin - Michigan
- Alan Lowenthal - California
- Nita Lowey – New York

- Jerrold Nadler – New York
- Jared Polis - Colorado
- Janice Schakowsky – Illinois, chief deputy whip for the Democratic Party
- Adam Schiff - California
- Brad Schneider - Illinois
- Debbie Wasserman Schultz – Florida, chairwoman of the Democratic National Committee
- Allyson Schwartz - Pennsylvania
- Bradley Sherman - California
- Henry Waxman - California

–Republicans:

- Eric Cantor – Virginia, Republican majority leader

Note that thirteen of the twenty-two Jewish representatives listed, or fifty-nine percent, are from three of the four most important states in the Electoral College (California, New York, and Florida) – this despite the fact that Jews comprise just 3.3 percent of California's population, just 8.4 percent of New York's population, and just 3.4 percent of Florida's population.[31]

<u>Supreme Court</u> – The highest court in America, the Supreme Court has final say on many of the social issues that affect our daily lives, which include such topics as abortion, affirmative action, and same-sex marriage. **Three of our nine current Supreme Court justices, or thirty-three percent, are Jewish** and include:

- Stephen Breyer – San Francisco – Appointed by Bill Clinton
- Ruth Bader Ginsberg – New York City – Appointed by Bill Clinton
- Elena Kagan – New York City – Appointed by Barack Obama

Note that these three justices were all appointed by Democrats, are all from ultra-liberal American cities, and are all considered to represent the liberal wing of the Supreme Court.

### *Federally Funded Research and Development Centers (FFRDCs)*

FFRDCs are the governmental equivalent of private sector think tanks. Unlike think tanks, however, FFRDCS are funded by the government. As such, they can be realistically viewed as agencies of the government. FFRDCs have a massive impact on the policies enacted by the federal government itself. **The following FFRDCs are among the most important and all have Jewish chairmen and CEOs:**

Center for Naval Analyses
Key Figure: Robert Murray, CEO
–Conducts research for the United States Navy and the United States Marine Corps in an effort to improve national defense

Lawrence Livermore National Laboratory
Key Figure: Norman Pattiz, chairman
–Conducts research for the Department of Energy in regard to ensuring the safety of America's nuclear arsenal

Los Alamos National Laboratory
Key Figure: Norman Pattiz, chairman
–Conducts research for the Department of Energy for the creation of nuclear weapons

Mitre Corporation
Key Figure: James R. Schlesinger, chairman
Mitre Corporation manages the following FFRDCs:

- Center for Advanced Aviation Systems Development – Conducts research for the Federal Aviation Administration

- Center for Enterprise Modernization – Conducts research for the Internal Revenue Service and Veterans Administration
- Homeland Security Systems Engineering and Development Institute – Conducts research for the Department of Homeland Security
- National Security Engineering Center – Conducts research for the Department of Defense and focuses on national security issues

National Cancer Institute
Key Figure: Harold Varmus, director
–Conducts cancer research for the Department of Health and Human Services

Princeton Plasma Physics Laboratory
Key Figure: Stewart Prager, director
–Conducts research in plasma physics and nuclear fusion for the Department of Energy

Rand Corporation
Key Figure: Michael Rich, CEO
Rand Corporation manages the following FFRDCs:

- Arroyo Center – Conducts research for the United States Army
- National Defense Research Institute – Conducts research for the Department of Defense, the United States Marine Corps, and the United States Navy
- Project Air Force – Conducts research and analysis for the United States Air Force

Science and Technology Policy Institute
Key Figure: Mark Lewis, director

–Conducts research in science and technology for the National Science Foundation

### Governing America's Biggest Cities

It is important to note that the administrations of many of the most important cities in the United States are headed by men and women of Jewish origin. **According to the 2010 census, thirty-three cities had populations of half a million or more people.**[32] **No less than five of these thirty-three cities, or fifteen percent, have Jewish mayors** and they include:

- Jonathan Rothschild – Democrat, Tucson
- Carolyn Goodman – Independent, Las Vegas
- Michael Bloomberg – Independent, New York City
- Rahm Emanuel – Democrat, Chicago
- Bob Filner – Independent, San Diego

**Michael Bloomberg and Rahm Emmanuel are the respective Jewish mayors of two of the three largest cities in America, New York City (8.3 million people) and Chicago (2.7 million people).**[33]

In particular, it is crucial to note the history of Jewish influence in New York City, the most populous and important city in the United States of America. New York City is the world's largest Jewish enclave outside of Israel itself, yet Jews still represent less than fifteen percent of the city's population (by the most liberal estimates). Nonetheless, **three of New York City's past five mayors, or sixty percent, have been Jewish** and include:

- Michael Bloomberg – Independent, current mayor of New York City
- Ed Koch – Democrat, former mayor of New York City

- Abraham Beame – Democrat, former mayor of New York City

The three above-listed men have combined to serve as mayor of New York City for twenty-eight of the past forty years.

# JEWS IN LAW

Anti-defamation leagues, civil rights groups, and law centers play a highly important role in American society. These various organizations claim to be upholders of the law, protectors of the rights of private citizens, and fighters of discrimination. And while this is true to some extent, these groups are also free to pick and choose the causes they support, which, more often than not, are liberal in nature. This is not surprising as **the presidents, directors, and chairmen of the most prominent of America's law associations, as we shall now see, are exclusively Jewish.**

### *Important Law Organizations and their Jewish Leaders*

*American Center for Law and Justice*

- Jay Sekulow – Chief Counsel

"The American Center for Law and Justice (ACLJ) and its globally affiliated organizations are committed to ensuring the ongoing viability of freedom and liberty in the United States and around the world. By focusing on U.S. Constitutional law, European Union law and human rights law, the ACLJ and its affiliated organizations are dedicated to the concept that freedom and liberty are universal, God-given and inalienable rights that must be protected."[34]

*American Civil Liberties Union*

- Susan Herman – President

"The ACLU is our nation's guardian of liberty, working daily in courts, legislatures and communities to defend and preserve the individual rights and liberties that the Constitution and laws of the United States guarantee everyone in this country."[35]

*Anti-Defamation League*

- Abraham Foxman – Director

"The Anti-Defamation League was founded in 1913 to stop the defamation of the Jewish people and to secure justice and fair treatment to all. Now the nation's premier civil rights/human relations agency, ADL fights anti-Semitism and all forms of bigotry, defends democratic ideals and protects civil rights for all."[36]

*Human Rights Watch*

- Kenneth Roth – Director

"Human Rights Watch is one of the world's leading independent organizations dedicated to defending and protecting human rights. By focusing international attention where human rights are violated, we give voice to the oppressed and hold oppressors accountable for their crimes."[37]

*Leadership Conference on Civil and Human Rights*

- Judith Lichtman – Chairman

"The Leadership Conference on Civil and Human Rights is a coalition charged by its diverse membership of more than two hundred national organizations to promote and protect the civil and human rights of all persons in the United States."[38]

*Southern Poverty Law Center*

- Richard Cohen – President

"The Southern Poverty Law Center is dedicated to fighting hate and bigotry, and to seeking justice for the most vulnerable members of our society. Using litigation, education and other forms of advocacy, we work toward the day when the ideals of equal justice and equal opportunity will be a reality."[39]

# JEWS IN ACADEMIA

For our purposes, "academia" includes the nation's elite universities, its powerful think tanks, and its influential intelligentsia. The men and women that comprise these groups wield enormous power in that they can influence the way we think, the way tomorrow's leaders think, and the manner in which policy-decisions are made by the federal government. Not surprisingly, the collective influence of America's intellectuals has been singularly liberal in nature, questioning the established order that led to our nation's rise as the world's preeminent superpower. The Ivory Tower, it must be said, is no friend of America's, a point that the late William F. Buckley, Jr. began making in the 1950s.[40]

### The Ivy League

Brown University, Columbia University, Cornell University, Dartmouth College, Harvard University, Princeton University, the University of Pennsylvania, and Yale University, which comprise the Ivy League, represent the pinnacle of higher education in America. Yet for all the proclamations of the benefits of diversity and open-mindedness tossed down from the Ivory Tower, the Ivy League is singularly Jewish, as an analysis of these eight institutions reveals. Nearly all of these institutions have Jewish-influenced histories in terms of the presidents installed to oversee their daily workings, as well as in terms of their most prominent and influential professors. It is difficult to understand how a handful of people coming from the same exclusive background and controlling our most elite institutions of learning can be beneficial for a country which, otherwise, is so amazingly diverse. Note that **not less than five of the eight Ivy League schools, or sixty-three percent, currently have Jewish presidents**.

*Brown University* – Recent Jewish presidents of Brown University include:

- None – However, Chancellor Thomas Tisch is Jewish

–Brown University's most prominent faculty members include the following Jewish professors:

- Leon Cooper – Physicist, recipient of the 1972 Nobel Prize in Physics
- Oded Galor – Economist, co-director of the National Bureau of Economic Research Committee on Income Distribution
- John Kosterlitz – Physicist, fellow of the American Physical Society
- Martha Nussbaum – Philosopher and feminist, winner of multiple writing awards

*Columbia University* – Recent Jewish presidents of Columbia University include:

- Lee Bollinger – 2002-Present
- Michael Sovern – 1980-1993

–Columbia University's most prominent faculty members include the following Jewish professors:

- Ronald Breslow – Chemist, winner of the 1991 National Medal of Science

- David Freedberg – Art historian, emphasis on the Dutch Masters
- Milos Forman – Film director, winner of Academy Awards in 1975 and 1984
- Brian Greene – Theoretical physicist, noted for work in string theory
- Joseph Stiglitz – Economist, recipient of the 2001 Nobel Prize in Economic Sciences

*Cornell University* – Recent Jewish presidents of Cornell University include:

- David Skorton – 2006-Present
- Jeffrey Lehman – 2003-2006

–Cornell University's most prominent faculty members include the following Jewish professors:

- Paul Ginsparg – Theoretical physicist, fellow of the American Physical Society
- Paul Greengard – Neuroscientist, recipient of the 2000 Nobel Prize for Physiology or Medicine
- Roald Hoffmann –Theoretical chemist, recipient of the 1981 Nobel Prize in Chemistry
- Michal Lipson – Physicist, known for advanced work in silicon photonics

*Dartmouth College* – Recent Jewish presidents of Dartmouth College include:

- James Freedman – 1987-1998
- John Kemeny – 1970-1981

–Dartmouth College's most prominent faculty members include the following Jewish professors:

- Lawrence Kritzman - Writer, emphasis on French culture and politics
- Jaron Lanier – Computer scientist, pioneer in virtual reality technology
- Jerry Zaks – Theater director, three-time Tony Award winner

*Harvard University* – Recent Jewish presidents of Harvard University include:

- Lawrence Summers – 2001-2006
- Neil Rudenstine – 1991-2001

–Harvard University's most prominent faculty members include the following Jewish professors:

- Alan Dershowitz – Professor of law, renowned defender of Israel
- Martin Feldstein – Economist, emeritus of the National Bureau of Economic Research
- Al Franken – Politician, popular voice of now-defunct Air America radio
- Alyssa Goodman – Astronomer, founder of the Harvard Initiative in Innovative Computing
- Roy Glauber – Theoretical physicist, recipient of the 2005 Nobel Prize in Physics
- Stephen Greenblatt – Literary critic, founder of the New Historicism movement
- Stanley Hoffman – Political scientist, author of multiple books on American foreign policy
- Lawrence Lessig – Philosopher, has called for a second Constitutional Convention

- Robert Levin – Professor of classical music, re-constructor of unfinished works by Bach and Mozart
- Stephen Marglin – Economist, member of the World Future Council
- Steven Pinker – Psychologist, proponent of evolutionary psychology
- Michael Rabin – Computer scientist, winner of the Turing Award
- Michael Sandel – Philosopher, advocate of Communitarianism

*Princeton University* – Recent Jewish presidents of Princeton University include:

- Christopher Eisgruber – 2013-Present
- Harold Tafler Shapiro – 1988-2001

–Princeton University's most prominent faculty members include the following Jewish professors:

- Orley Ashenfelter – Economist, winner of the Frisch Medal
- Charles Beitz – Political scientist, fellow of the American Academy of Arts and Sciences
- Jan Gross – Historian, focus on Jewish history
- Daniel Kahneman – Psychologist, recipient of the 2002 Nobel Prize in Economic Sciences
- Alan Krueger – Economist, former assistant secretary of the Treasury
- Paul Krugman – Journalist, recipient of the 2008 Nobel Prize in Economic Sciences
- Daniel Kurtzer – Political scientist, former United States ambassador to Israel
- Paul Lewis – Architect, winner of the Mercedes T. Bass Rome Prize

- Harvey Rosen – Economist, former chairman of the Council of Economic Advisers
- Peter Singer – Philosopher, noted supporter of animal rights

*University of Pennsylvania* – Recent Jewish presidents of the University of Pennsylvania include:

- Amy Gutmann – 2004-Present
- Judith Rodin – 1994-2004
- Claire Fagin – 1993-1994
- Martin Myerson – 1970-1981

–The University of Pennsylvania's most prominent faculty members include the following Jewish professors:

- Ralph Brinster – Geneticist, winner of the 2010 National Medal of Science
- Steven Hahn – Historian, winner of the 2005 Pulitzer Prize in History
- Alan Kors – Historian, winner of the 2005 National Humanities Medal

*Yale University* – Recent Jewish presidents of Yale University include:

- Richard Levin – 1993-Present

–Yale University's most prominent faculty members include the following Jewish professors:

- Sidney Altman – Molecular biologist, recipient of the 1989 Nobel Prize in Chemistry
- Harold Bloom – Literary critic, expert on the complete works of William Shakespeare

- David Gelertner – Computer scientist, fellow in Jewish Thought at the Shalem Center
- Donald Kagan – Historian, winner of the 2002 National Humanities Medal
- Herbert Scarf – Economist, fellow of the American Academy of Arts and Sciences
- Robert Shiller – Economist, creator of the Case-Shiller real estate index
- Joan Steitz – Molecular biologist, noted for work in ribonucleic acids
- Thomas Steitz – Professor of biophysics and biochemistry, recipient of the 2009 Nobel Prize in Chemistry

## Think Tanks

The private sector version of the FFRDCs discussed earlier, think tanks are organizations that advocate for their preferred positions on topics such as civil liberties, economics, and foreign affairs. Though not funded by the federal government, think tanks have just as much influence on the policy-making process in America, if not more, as FFRDCs. **An analysis of the top fifty American think tanks, as ranked by the University of Pennsylvania, shows that twenty-five, or fifty percent, have Jewish leaders**, and they include the following:[41]

Aspen Institute
Key Figure: Walter Isaacson, CEO
Primary Focus: "fostering enlightened leadership"

Carnegie Council for Ethics in International Affairs
Key Figure: Joel Rosenthal, president
Primary Focus: international affairs

Carnegie Endowment for International Peace
Key Figure: Jessica Matthews, president
Primary Focus: foreign policy

Cato Institute
Key Figure: Robert A. Levy, chairman
Primary Focus: civil liberties

Center on Budget and Policy Priorities
Key Figure: Robert Greenstein, president
Primary Focus: budget and tax policy

Center for International Development
Key Figure: Ricardo Hausmann, director
Primary Focus: global poverty

Center for the National Interest
Key Figure: Maurice Greenberg, chairman
Primary Focus: foreign affairs

Center for a New American Security
Key Figure: Richard Fontaine, president
Primary Focus: national security

Council on Foreign Relations
Key Figure: Richard Haass, president
Primary Focus: foreign policy

Earth Institute
Key Figure: Jeffrey Sachs, director
Primary Focus: climate change

Economic Policy Institute
Key Figure: Lawrence Mishel, president
Primary Focus: economic policy

Foreign Policy Research Institute
Key Figure: Alan Luxenberg, president
Primary Focus: foreign policy

Freedom House
Key Figure: David Cramer, president
Primary Focus: civil liberties

Hudson Institute
Key Figure: Kenneth Weinstein, CEO
Primary Focus: global security

Human Rights Watch
Key Figure: Kenneth Roth, chairman
Primary Focus: human rights

Inter-American Dialogue
Key Figure: Michael Shifter, president
Primary Focus: Western Hemisphere affairs

Open Society Foundation
Key Figure: George Soros, chairman
Primary Focus: democratic governance

Pew Center on Global Climate Change (Center for Climate and Energy Solutions)
Key Figure: Eileen Claussen, president
Primary Focus: climate and energy solutions

Pew Research Center
Key Figure: Donald Kimmelman, chairman
Primary Focus: public opinion polling

Manhattan Institute
Key Figure: Paul Singer, chairman
Primary Focus: economic choice and individual responsibility

Mercatus Center
Key Figure: Tyler Cowen, director
Primary Focus: economics

Rand Corporation
Key Figure: Michael Rich, president
Primary Focus: national security

Urban Institute
Key Figure: Sarah Rosen Wartell, president
Primary Focus: economic and social issues

Woodrow Wilson International Center for Scholars
Key Figure: Joseph Gildenhorn, chairman
Primary Focus: humanities and social sciences

World Resources Institute
Key Figure: James Harmon, chairman
Primary Focus: environmental issues

*Intellectuals*

**A recent ranking of the world's one hundred greatest living intellectuals included thirty-six Americans, of whom twenty-two, or sixty-one percent, are Jewish.**[42] The obvious concern, for our purposes, is the domination of thought by such a small and homogenous group of individuals. For the twenty-two Jewish intellectuals listed below are also dominant in their respective fields of endeavor.

- Noam Chomsky – Linguist, most frequently cited living scholar
- Jared Diamond – Scientist, winner of the 2008 Pulitzer Prize in General Non-Fiction
- Paul Ekman – Psychologist, noted for advanced work in understanding facial expressions
- Thomas Friedman – Journalist, expert in Middle East affairs
- Howard Gardner – Psychologist, noted for theory of multiple intelligences

- Neil Gershenfeld – Physicist, influential writer on modern technology
- Robert Kagan – Foreign policy adviser, co-founder of the now-defunct Project for the New American Century
- Daniel Kahneman - Psychologist, recipient of the 2002 Nobel Prize in Economic Sciences
- Paul Krugman – Journalist, recipient of the 2008 Nobel Prize in Economic Sciences
- Jaron Lanier - Computer scientist, pioneer in virtual reality technology
- Lawrence Lessig - Philosopher, has called for a second Constitutional Convention
- Bernard Lewis – Historian, expert in Middle East affairs
- Martha Nussbaum - Philosopher and feminist, winner of multiple writing awards
- Steven Pinker – Psychologist, proponent of evolutionary psychology
- Richard Posner – Jurist, most frequently cited living legal scholar
- Robert Putnam – Political scientist, known for ground-breaking two-level game theory
- Jeffrey Sachs – Economist, advisor to the IMF, World Bank, and the World Health Organization
- Lawrence Summers – Economist, former secretary of the treasury
- Harold Varmus – Director of the National Cancer Institute, recipient of the 1989 Nobel Prize for Physiology or Medicine
- Michael Walzer – Political philosopher, advocate of Communitarianism
- Steven Weinberg – Theoretical physicist, recipient of the 1979 Nobel Prize in Physics
- Paul Wolfowitz – Former deputy secretary of defense, driving force behind American invasion of Iraq in 2003

# JEWS IN THE MEDIA

The idea that the national news media has a liberal bias is not just a figment of the collective conservative imagination, but rather the indisputable truth. A recent study, the first of its kind, was undertaken by a group of UCLA professors that actually quantified liberal bias in the American media. The results of the study appeared in a 2005 issue of the *Quarterly Journal of Economics*.[43] Eighteen of the twenty major media outlets analyzed in the study were deemed as having a clear liberal bent. Meanwhile, the few news outlets that cater to conservatives, such as Fox News Channel, suffer the most unimaginable and vitriolic attacks from the political left. It is almost as if the mere existence of a single conservative media outlet is too much for some liberals to bear. Sadly, this is but one more example proving the fallacy of supposed liberal open-mindedness. But the obvious problem of such liberal domination of the media is the closing off to the average American of what should be a much wider array of opinions and ideas. As the situation currently stands, the liberal media has nearly total control over how the country's news is reported.

### Newspapers & Magazines

#### Top Twenty-Five Daily Newspapers in America

The country's top twenty-five daily newspapers bring the political news of the world to citizens across America and have the power to put whatever spin on said news they so desire. Circulations for these newspapers range from 225,000 – 2,294,000 copies each day.[44] **No less than fourteen of America's top twenty-five daily newspapers, or fifty-six percent, are owned, published, or edited by Jews. More telling, the three largest and most influential daily newspapers in the United States, the *Wall Street Journal*, *USA Today*, and the *New York Times*, are all owned and operated by American Jews**.

- *Boston Globe*: owned by New York Times Co. (Arthur Sulzberger, Jr., chairman)
- *Chicago Tribune*: owned by Tribune Company (Bruce Karsh, chairman)
- *Cleveland Plain Dealer*: owned by S.I. Newhouse family
- *Houston Chronicle*: edited by Jeff Cohen
- *Los Angeles Times*: published by Eddy Hartenstein
- *New York Daily News*: published by Mortimer Zuckerman
- *New York Post*: owned by News Corporation (Rupert Murdoch, CEO)
- *New York Times*: owned by New York Times Co. (Arthur Sulzberger, Jr., chairman)
- *Newark Star-Ledger*: owned by S.I. Newhouse family
- *Orange County Register*: published by Aaron Kushner
- *Oregonian*: owned by S.I. Newhouse family
- *USA Today*: published by Larry Kramer
- *Wall Street Journal*: owned by News Corporation (Rupert Murdoch, CEO)
- *Washington Post*: owned by Washington Post Company (Donald Graham, CEO)

*–New York Times Leadership*

The leadership of the *New York Times* is particularly deserving of attention because of the newspaper's unparalleled influence and overwhelmingly Jewish management:

- Arthur Sulzberger, Jr. – chairman and publisher
- Michael Golden – vice chairman
- Jill Abramson – executive editor

## Major Magazines

**Many of the most popular American magazines are owned, published, or edited by Jewish-Americans** and they include the following:

- *Bloomberg Business Week*: Joshua Tyrangiel, editor
- *Car and Driver*: Eddie Alterman, editor
- *Men's Journal*: Jann Wenner, owner
- *New York Magazine*: Adam Moss, editor
- *New York Times Magazine*: Arthur Sulzberger, Jr., owner
- *The New Yorker*: David Remnick, editor
- *Rolling Stone*: Jann Wenner, editor
- *Time Magazine*: Richard Stengel, editor
- *US News & World Report*: Mortimer Zuckerman, owner
- *US Weekly*: Jann Wenner, owner
- *Weekly Standard*: William Kristol, editor
- *Wine Spectator*: Marvin Shanken, publisher and editor

*Reporters & Journalists*

**The most famous and influential names in American journalism are nearly all Jewish** and include:

- David Brooks – *New York Times*
- Carl Bernstein – *Washington Post*
- Thomas Friedman – *New York Times*
- Paul Krugman – *New York Times*
- Seymour Hirsch – *New York Times*
- David Remnick – *Washington Post*
- Robert Novak – *Wall Street Journal*

- Judith Miller – *New York Times*
- Matthew Drudge – *Drudge Report*
- Jonah Goldberg – *USA Today*
- George F. Will – *Washington Post*

*Jewish Reporters with Syndicated Columns*

The syndication of any reporter's column multiplies that reporter's influence to an exponential degree. **A recent report listed a total of sixty-nine newspaper columns being syndicated throughout the United States, of which twenty, or twenty-nine percent, are written by Jewish journalists.**[45]

- Max Boot, writes for *Los Angeles Times*
- Jonathan Chait, writes for *Los Angeles Times*
- Susan Estrich, writes for *USA Today*
- David Frum, writes for *The National Post*
- Stuart Goldman, writes for *Los Angeles Times*
- Amira Hass, writes for *Ha'aretz*
- Nat Hentoff, writes for *Wall Street Journal*
- Naomi Klein, writes for *The Globe and Mail*
- Dave Kopel, writes for *National Review*
- Charles Krauthammer, writes for *Weekly Standard*
- Rich Lowry, writes for *National Review*
- Jeanne Phillips, writes for *Universal Press Syndicate*
- Melanie Phillips, writes for *The Daily Mail*
- Daniel Pipes, writes for *The Jerusalem Post*
- Katha Pollitt, writes for *The Nation*
- Ted Rall, writes for *Universal Press Syndicate*
- Jeffrey Seglin, writes for *Tribune Media Services*
- Ben Shapiro, writes for *Creators Syndicate*
- Mark Steyn, writes for *The Daily Telegraph*
- John Stossel, writes for *Creators Syndicate*

## *The Internet*

In the modern era, America's youngest billionaires are largely building their personal fortunes by exploiting the power of the internet. Millions of Americans now communicate, shop, and work online. The ability to influence via the internet is endless, yet cost-effective. And **America's Jews have a near monopoly on the most powerful websites in existence**.

- Facebook
  Segment: online social networking
  Key Figure: Mark Zuckerberg, chairman & CEO

- Google
  Segment: internet search engine
  Key Figure: Sergey Brin, co-CEO
  Key Figure: Larry Page, co-CEO

- LinkedIn
  Segment: online business networking
  Key Figure: Reid Hoffman, chairman

- Wikipedia
  Segment: online encyclopedia
  Key Figure: Jimmy Wales, founder

## *Television News*

Television is a hugely important medium through which millions of Americans receive their news, which includes economic, political, and social happenings. Those who doubt that television news is politically charged need only be reminded of the multiple news reporting scandals that took place on major networks during the administration of George W. Bush, the most notorious of which involved Dan Rather (not Jewish).

## Top Network Channels

Amazingly, **all four of the major broadcasting networks in the United States, or one hundred percent, are controlled by American Jews**.

- <u>American Broadcasting Company (ABC)</u>
  Owned by Walt Disney Company
  Key Figure: Bob Iger, chairman & CEO

- <u>Columbia Broadcasting System (CBS)</u>
  Owned by the CBS Corporation
  Key Figure: Sumner Redstone, chairman
  Key Figure: Leslie Moonves, CEO

- <u>Fox Broadcasting Company (FOX)</u>
  Owned by News Corporation
  Key Figure: Rupert Murdoch, chairman & CEO

- <u>National Broadcasting Company (NBC)</u>
  Owned by Comcast Corporation
  Key Figure: Brian Roberts, chairman & CEO

## Top Cable News Channels

Cable news is no less influenced by Jewish-Americans than public network news. In fact, **all three of the highest rated cable news channels in America, or one hundred percent, are headed by Jews**.[46]

- <u>Cable News Network (CNN)</u>
  Key Figure: Jeffrey Zucker, president

- Fox News Channel
  Owned by News Corporation
  Key Figure: Rupert Murdoch, chairman & CEO

- Microsoft and the National Broadcasting Company
  (MSNBC)
  Owned by Comcast Corporation
  Key Figure: Brian Roberts, CEO

*Jewish Broadcasters, Newscasters, and Pundits*

While difficult to quantity, it can be safely stated that **Jews domi-nate the ranks of America's most famous and influential newscasters** on both public news networks and cable news channels.

- Marv Albert – Sports News
- Chris Berman – Sports News
- Wolf Blitzer – Political News
- Liz Cho – Political News
- Connie Chung – Political News
- Alan Colmes – Political News
- Katie Couric – Political News
- Jim Cramer – Financial News
- David Faber – Financial News
- Larry King – Political News
- Ted Koppel – Political News
- Larry Kudlow – Financial News
- Matt Lauer – Political News
- Bill Maher – Political News
- Al Michaels – Sports News
- Gabe Pressman – Political News
- Geraldo Rivera – Political News
- Morley Safer – Political News
- Jeremy Schaap – Sports News
- Adam Schefter – Sports News

- Tabitha Soren – Political News
- Jon Stewart – Political News
- John Stossel – Political News
- Chris Wallace – Political News
- Barbara Walters – Political News
- Warner Wolf – Sports News

## *Radio*

The advent of television was the death knell for radio as a cherished forum for news in the lives of Americans. However, millions of people still listen to radio broadcasting in their cars and at work for all types of news and programming. And **the largest and most important radio stations are predominantly owned and operated by Jewish-Americans**.

Major American Radio Corporations

- Bloomberg Business News
  Owned by Bloomberg LP
  Key Figure: Michael Bloomberg, owner

- Fox News Radio
  Owned by News Corporation
  Key Figure: Rupert Murdoch, chairman & CEO

- Oaktree Capital Management, LP
  Owns the CBS Radio Network, the NBC Radio Network, and Westwood One Radio
  Key Figure: Howard Marks, chairman
  Key Figure: Bruce Karsh, president

- Sirius XM Satellite Radio
  Benefits from a virtual monopoly in satellite radio broadcasting

Key Figure: Eddy Hartenstein, chairman
Key Figure: Mel Karmazin, CEO

- <u>Walt Disney Company</u>
  Owns ABC News Radio, ESPN Radio, and Radio Disney
  Key Figure: Bob Iger, chairman & CEO

*Jewish Radio Personalities*

**America's most famous radio personalities have always been, and continue to be, primarily Jewish.**

- Al Franken – "The Al Franken Show"
- Don Imus – "Imus in the Morning"
- Mark Levin – "The Mark Levin Show"
- Michael Savage – "The Savage Nation"
- Dr. Laura Schlessinger – "The Dr. Laura Program"
- Howard Stern – "The Howard Stern Show"

# JEWS IN BUSINESS

Jewish influence within America's largest corporations remains consistently strong, which is crucially important. Controlling a corporation means controlling thousands of jobs, controlling lobbying efforts, and controlling political campaign donations.

The *Fortune* 500 is the preeminent annual ranking of the largest corporations in the United States. Combined, the corporations listed therein control millions of jobs and trillions of dollars in revenue. The *Fortune* 100, of course, is the cream of the crop among these corporations in terms of power and influence. **Analysis of the *Fortune* 100 for 2012 shows that no less than nineteen of these one hundred elite corporations, or nineteen percent, are under Jewish management at their respective pinnacles.**[47]

### *Jewish Influence in Corporate America*

*The following corporate members of the Fortune 100 retain Jewish chairmen and CEOs:*

- American International Group (AIG)
  Industry: insurance
  Key Figure: Robert Benmosche, president & CEO

- **Apple, Inc.**
  Industry: computers
  Key Figure: Arthur Levinson, chairman

- **CHS, Inc.**
  Industry: agriculture
  Key Figure: David Bielenberg, chairman

- **Comcast Corporation**
  Industry: telecommunications, mass media
  Key Figure: Brian Roberts, chairman & CEO

- **Costco Wholesale Corporation**
  Industry: retailing
  Key Figure: Jeffrey Brotman, chairman

- **Deere & Company**
  Industry: heavy equipment
  Key Figure: Samuel Allen, chairman & CEO

- **Dell, Inc.**
  Industry: computers
  Key Figure: Michael Dell, CEO

- **Google, Inc.**
  Industry: internet
  Key Figure: Sergey Brin, co-CEO
  Key Figure: Larry Page, co-CEO

- **The Goldman Sachs Group, Inc.**
  Industry: banking
  Key Figure: Lloyd Blankfein, chairman & CEO

- **Hess Corporation**
  Industry: oil
  Key Figure: John Hess, chairman & CEO

- Home Depot
  Industry: retailing
  Key Figure: Arthur Blank, founder

- Lowe's Companies, Inc.
  Industry: retailing
  Key Figure: James Tisch, CEO

- Medco Health Solutions, Inc.
  Industry: healthcare
  Key Figure: Kenneth Klepper, CEO

- Microsoft Corporation
  Industry: software
  Key Figure: Steve Ballmer, CEO

- News Corporation
  Industry: mass media
  Key Figure: Rupert Murdoch, chairman & CEO

- Oracle Corporation
  Industry: software
  Key Figure: Larry Ellison, CEO

- Prudential Financial, Inc.
  Industry: financial services
  Key Figure: John Strangfeld, Jr., chairman & CEO

- Sears Holdings Corporation
  Industry: retailing
  Key Figure: Edward Lampert, chairman & CEO

- Walt Disney Company
  Industry: mass media
  Key Figure: Bob Iger, chairman & CEO

*Beyond the Fortune 100* - The following corporations, well-known to the average American, also retain Jewish chairmen and CEOs:

- **Alcoa, Inc.**
  Industry: metals
  Key Figure: Klaus Kleinfeld, chairman & CEO

- **Bed Bath & Beyond, Inc.**
  Industry: retail
  Key Figure: Warren Eisenberg, co-chairmen
  Key Figure: Leonard Feinstein, co-chairmen

- **Bloomberg LP**
  Industry: financial news media
  Key Figure: Michael Bloomberg, owner

- **Caesars Entertainment Corporation**
  Industry: hospitality, tourism
  Key Figure: Gary Loveman, CEO

- **Estee Lauder Companies**
  Industry: personal care
  Key Figure: William Lauder, chairman

- **Family Dollar Stores**
  Industry: retail
  Key Figure: Howard Levine, chairman & CEO

- **Genentech, Inc.**
  Industry: biotechnology
  Key Figure: Arthur Levinson, chairman

- **Goodyear Tire and Rubber Company**
  Industry: manufacturing
  Key Figure: Richard Kramer, chairman & CEO

- Las Vegas Sands Corporation
  Industry: hospitality, tourism
  Key Figure: Sheldon Adelson, chairman & CEO

- MacAndrew & Forbes Holdings, Inc.
  Industry: diversified
  Key Figure: Ron Perelman, chairman & CEO

- Marvel Entertainment, LLC
  Industry: entertainment
  Key Figure: Isaac Perlmutter, CEO

- PNC Financial Services
  Industry: financial services
  Key Figure: Jim Rohr, chairman & CEO

- Qualcomm, Inc.
  Industry: telecommunications
  Key Figure: Paul Jacobs, CEO

- Seagram Company Ltd
  Industry: alcoholic beverages
  Key Figure: Charles Bronfman, CEO

- Starbucks Corporation
  Industry: restaurants
  Key Figure: Howard Schulz, chairman & CEO

- Tesoro Corporation
  Industry: oil
  Key Figure: Steven Grapstein, chairman

- The TJX Companies, Inc.
  Industry: retail
  Key Figure: Carol Meyrowitz, CEO

- <u>Toys "R" Us, Inc.</u>
  Industry: retail
  Key Figure: Gerald Storch, chairman & CEO

- <u>The Travelers Companies</u>
  Industry: insurance
  Key Figure: Jay Fishman, chairman & CEO

- <u>Viacom, Inc.</u>
  Industry: mass media
  Key Figure: Summer Redstone, chairman

- <u>Waste Management Inc.</u>
  Industry: waste management
  Key Figure: David Steiner, CEO

- <u>Yum! Brands, Inc.</u>
  Industry: restaurants
  Key Figure: David Novak, chairman & CEO

*Disgraced CEOs No Longer in Power* - Several Jewish CEOs, listed below, became pariahs during the Great Recession and are no longer in power.

- <u>American International Group, Inc. (AIG)</u>
  Industry: insurance
  Key Figure: Maurice Greenberg, former chairman & CEO

- <u>Bernard L. Madoff Investment Securities, LLC</u>
  Industry: financial services
  Key Figure: Bernie Madoff, former chairman

- <u>Lehman Brothers Holdings, Inc.</u>
  Industry: financial services
  Key Figure: Richard Fuld, Jr., former chairman & CEO

## *Jews in Hedge Funds & Private Equity Groups*

While becoming the CEO of Goldman Sachs or JP Morgan obviously has its privileges, the true wealth, as the *Forbes* 400 indicates, is accrued by the managers of America's elite hedge funds and private equity groups. The men in charge of running these organizations, nearly exclusively Jewish, each control hundreds of billions of dollars in assets, a percentage of which ends up in their own pockets.

## Hedge Funds

**Analysis of a recent ranking of the top thirty hedge funds (by assets under management) in the United States shows that twenty-two, or seventy-three percent, are managed by men of Jewish origin.**[48]

- Appaloosa Management: David Tepper, CEO
- Avenue Capital Group: Marc Lasry, CEO
- Carlyle Group: David Rubenstein, co-CEO
- Caxton Associates: Bruce Kovner, chairman
- Elliot Management Corporation: Paul Singer, CEO
- ESL Investments: Edward Lampert, CEO
- Farallon Capital Management: Tom Steyer, CEO
- Greenlight Capital: David Einhorn, CEO
- Highbridge Capital Management: Glenn Dubin, CEO
- Icahn Enterprises: Carl Icahn, CEO
- Lone Pine Capital: Stephen Mandel, CEO
- Millennium Management: Israel Englander, CEO
- Och-Ziff Capital Management: Daniel Och, CEO
- Omega Advisors: Leon Cooperman, CEO
- Paulson & Co: John Paulson, president
- Pershing Square Capital Management: Bill Ackman, CEO
- Renaissance Technologies: James Simons, CEO
- SAC Capital Advisors: Steve Cohen, CEO
- Soros Fund Management: George Soros, chairman

- Talpion Fund Management: Henry Swieca, CEO
- Third Point, LLC: Dan Loeb, CEO
- Trian Fund Management: Nelson Peltz, executive partner

Private Equity Groups

**Analysis of a recent ranking of the top thirty private equity groups (by capital raised) in the United States shows that nine, or thirty percent, are managed by men of Jewish origin.**[49]

- Apollo Global Management: Leon Black, managing partner
- Ares Management: David Sachs, senior advisor
- Blackstone Group: Stephen Schwarzman, CEO
- Cerberus Capital Management: Steve Feinberg, CEO
- Lindsay Goldberg: Alan Goldberg, co-managing partner
- NGP Energy Capital Management: Kenneth Hersh, CEO
- Oaktree Capital Management: Bruce Karsh, president
- Kohlberg Kravis Roberts: Henry Kravis and George Roberts, co-CEOs
- TPG Capital: David Bonderman, founding partner

*Jewish Billionaires*

The annual *Forbes* 400 is considered the definitive list of America's ultra-wealthy, separating celebrities worth a mere $500 million from the old money bluebloods and the titans of industry each worth at least $1 billion. **No less than one hundred thirty of the individuals to make the *Forbes* 400 in 2012, or thirty-three percent, are Jewish.**[50]

*Jewish-American Billionaires and their Sources of Wealth*

- S. Daniel Abraham – Dieting Products – Net Worth: $1.8 billion
- Sheldon Adelson – Casinos – Net Worth: $20.5 billion

- Paul Allen – Software – Net Worth: $15 billion
- Micky Arison – Cruises – Net Worth: $5 billion
- Ronald Baron – Private Equity – Net Worth: $1.5 billion
- Marc Benioff – Software – Net Worth: $2.2 billion
- Nicolas Berggruen – Investments – Net Worth: $2.3 billion
- Leon Black – Private Equity – Net Worth: $3.5 billion
- Arthur Blank – Retail – Net Worth: $1.5 billion
- Leonard Blavatnik – Diversified – Net Worth: $12.5 billion
- Michael Bloomberg – Mass Media – Net worth: $25 billion
- Neil Blumh – Real Estate – Net Worth: $2.1 billion
- David Bonderman – Private Equity – Net Worth: $2.6 billion
- Norman Braman – Car Dealerships – Net Worth: $1.6 billion
- Donald Bren – Real Estate – Net Worth: $13 billion
- Sergey Brin – Internet – Net Worth: $20.3 billion
- Eli Broad – Investments – Net Worth: $6.3 billion
- Leon Charney – Real Estate – Net Worth: $1.2 billion
- Steve Cohen – Hedge Funds – Net Worth: $8.8 billion
- Leon Cooperman – Hedge Funds – Net Worth: $2.2 billion
- Mark Cuban – Online Media – Net Worth: $2.3 billion
- Michael Dell – Computers – Net Worth: $14.6 billion
- Barry Diller – Mass Media – Net Worth: $1.8 billion
- Glenn Dubin – Hedge Funds – Net Worth: $1.7 billion
- David Einhorn – Hedge Funds – Net Worth: $1.2 billion
- Larry Ellison – Software – Net Worth: $41 billion
- Doris Fisher – Retail – Net Worth: $2.9 billion
- John Fisher – Retail – Net Worth: $2.3 billion
- Robert Fisher – Retail – Net Worth: $1.7 billion
- Robert Friedland – Mining – Net Worth: $1.3 billion
- Phillip Frost – Pharmaceuticals – Net Worth: $2.4 billion
- David Geffen – Music – Net Worth: $5.6 billion
- Malcolm Glazer – Investments – Net Worth: $3.6 billion

- Noam Gottesman – Hedge Funds – Net Worth: $1.7 billion
- David Gottesman – Investments – Net Worth: $1.7 billion
- Jeff Greene – Real Estate – Net Worth: $2.2 billion
- Joshua Harris – Private Equity – Net Worth: $1.6 billion
- Reid Hoffman – Internet – Net Worth: $2.1 billion
- James Irsay – Sports – Net Worth: $1.5 billion
- Carl Icahn – Leveraged Buyouts – Net Worth: $14.8 billion
- Irwin Jacobs – Telecommunications – Net Worth: $1.5 billion
- Jeremy Jacobs, Sr. – Sports – Net Worth: $2.7 billion
- George Kaiser – Oil – Net Worth: $10 billion
- Thomas Kaplan – Investments – Net Worth: $1.5 billion
- Bruce Karsh – Private Equity – Net Worth: $1.4 billion
- Sidney Kimmel – Retail – Net Worth: $1.2 billion
- Charles Koch – Diversified – Net Worth: $31 billion
- David Koch – Diversified – Net Worth: $31 billion
- Bruce Kovner – Hedge Funds – Net Worth: $4.3 billion
- Robert Kraft – Sports – Net Worth: $2.3 billion
- Henry Kravis – Leveraged Buyouts – Net Worth: $4 billion
- Edward Lampert – Hedge Funds – Net Worth: $3.2 billion
- Marc Lasry – Hedge Funds – Net Worth: $1.3 billion
- Leonard Lauder – Cosmetics – Net Worth: $7.7 billion
- Ronald Lauder – Cosmetics – Net Worth: $3.4 billion
- Ralph Lauren – Fashion – Net Worth: $6.5 billion
- Richard LeFrak – Real Estate – Net Worth: $5.2 billion
- Ted Lerner – Real Estate – Net Worth: $3.9 billion
- Peter B. Lewis – Insurance – Net Worth: $1.1 billion
- George Lindemann - Investments – Net Worth: $2.2 billion
- Daniel Loeb – Hedge Funds – Net Worth: $1.3 billion
- George Lucas – Movies – Net Worth: $3.3 billion
- Stephen Mandel, Jr. – Hedge Funds – Net Worth: $1.2 billion

- Bernard Marcus – Retail – Net Worth: $2.7 billion
- Howard Marks – Private Equity – Net Worth: $1.4 billion
- Gwendolyn Sontheim Meyer – Agriculture – Net Worth: $3 billion
- Michael Milken – Investments – Net Worth: $2.3 billion
- Michael Moritz – Venture Capital – Net Worth: $1.9 billion
- Dustin Moskovitz – Internet – Net Worth: $2.7 billion
- Rupert Murdoch – Mass Media – Net Worth: $9.4 billion
- Samuel Irving Newhouse, Jr. – Publishing – Net Worth: $7.4 billion
- Daniel Och – Hedge Funds – Net Worth: $2.3 billion
- Igor Olenicoff – Real estate – Net Worth: $2.4 billion
- Larry Page – Internet – Net Worth: $20.3 billion
- John Paulson – Hedge Funds – Net Worth: $11 billion
- Nelson Peltz – Hedge Funds – Net Worth: $1.2 billion
- Ron Perelman – Leveraged Buyouts – Net Worth: $12 billion
- Isaac Perlmutter – Entertainment – Net Worth: $2.3 billion
- Anthony Pritzker – Hotels – Net Worth: $2.5 billion
- Daniel Pritzker – Hotels – Net Worth: $1.7 billion
- James Pritzker – Hotels – Net Worth: $1.5 billion
- Jay Pritzker – Hotels – Net Worth: $2.5 billion
- Jean Pritzker – Hotels – Net Worth: $1.9 billion
- John Pritzker – Hotels – Net Worth: $1.8 billion
- Karen Pritzker – Hotels – Net Worth: $3.2 billion
- Linda Pritzker – Hotels – Net Worth: $1.6 billion
- Penny Pritzker – Hotels – Net Worth: $1.8 billion
- Thomas Pritzker – Hotels – Net Worth: $2.2 billion
- Stewart Rahr – Pharmaceuticals – Net Worth: $1.6 billion
- Mitchell Rales – Manufacturing – Net Worth: $3.4 billion
- Steven Rales – Manufacturing – Net Worth: $3.3 billion
- Sumner Redstone – Mass Media – Net Worth: $4.1 billion
- Ira Rennert – Investments – Net Worth: $6.5 billion

- Stewart Resnick – Agriculture – Net Worth: $2.2 billion
- Alexander Rovt – Fertilizer – Net Worth: $1.1 billion
- Marc Rowan – Private Equity – Net Worth: $1.5 billion
- George Roberts – Private Equity – Net Worth: $3.7 billion
- Stephen Ross – Real Estate – Net Worth: $4.4 billion
- David Rubenstein – Private Equity – Net Worth: $1.9 billion
- Haim Saban – Mass Media – Net Worth: $3.1 billion
- Henry Samueli – Semiconductors – Net Worth: $1.8 billion
- Howard Schultz – Coffee – Net Worth: $1.5 billion
- Lynn Schusterman – Oil – Net Worth: $3.5 billion
- Stephen Schwarzman – Private Equity – Net Worth: $5.2 billion
- Eugene Shvidler – Oil – Net Worth: $1.2 billion
- Herbert Simon – Real Estate – Net Worth: $2.2 billion
- James Simons – Hedge Funds – Net Worth: $11 billion
- Paul Singer – Hedge Funds – Net Worth: $1.1 billion
- Jeffrey Skoll – Internet – Net Worth: $3.3 billion
- Daniel Snyder – Sports – Net Worth: $1.1 billion
- Sheldon Solow – Real Estate – Net Worth: $3.5 billion
- George Soros – Hedge Funds – Net Worth: $19 billion
- Jerry Speyer – Real Estate – Net Worth: $3 billion
- Steven Speilberg – Movies – Net Worth: $3.2 billion
- Donald Sterling – Real Estate – Net Worth: $1.9 billion
- Leonard Stern – Real Estate – Net Worth: $4.2 billion
- Henry Swieca – Hedge Funds – Net Worth: $1.2 billion
- Alfred Taubman – Real Estate – Net Worth: $2.9 billion
- David Tepper – Hedge Funds – Net Worth: $5.5 billion
- Joan Tisch – Diversified – Net Worth: $2.7 billion
- Wilma Tisch – Diversified – Net Worth: $1.4 billion
- Les Wexner – Retail – Net Worth: $4.4 billion
- Steve Wynn – Casinos – Net Worth: $2.5 billion
- Sam Zell – Real Estate – Net Worth: $3.8 billion
- Daniel Ziff – Investments – Net Worth: $4.3 billion
- Dirk Ziff – Investments – Net Worth: $4.3 billion

- Robert Ziff – Investments – Net Worth: $4.3 billion
- Anita Zucker – Chemicals – Net Worth: $2.1 billion
- Mark Zuckerberg – Internet – Net Worth: $9.4 billion
- Mortimer Zuckerman – Real Estate – Net Worth: $2.4 billion

# JEWS IN REAL ESTATE

As the Great Recession has illustrated, real estate is the lasting source of wealth in America. And the vast majority of real estate is in the hands of American Jews. From individual tycoons to real estate investment trusts to publicly traded building corporations, Jews absolutely dominate real estate in the United States.

*Jewish Real Estate Tycoons*

**Of the 2012 *Forbes* 400, the wealth of twenty-four individuals came primarily from real estate – sixteen of those twenty-four men, or sixty-seven percent, are Jewish.**[51]

- Neil Bluhm – Net Worth: $2.1billion
- Donald Bren – Net Worth: $13 billion
- Leon Charney – Net Worth: $1.2 billion
- Jeff Greene – Net Worth: $2.2 billion
- Richard LeFrak – Net Worth: $5.2 billion
- Ted Lerner - Net Worth: $3.9 billion
- Igor Olenicoff – Net Worth: $2.4 billion
- Stephen Ross – Net Worth: $4.4 billion
- Herbert Simon – Net Worth: $2.2 billion
- Sheldon Solow – Net Worth: $3.5 billion

- Jerry Speyer – Net Worth: $3 billion
- Donald Sterling – Net Worth: $1.9 billion
- Leonard Stern – Net Worth: $4.2 billion
- Alfred Taubman – Net Worth: $2.9 billion
- Sam Zell – Net Worth: $3.8 billion
- Mortimer Zuckerman – Net Worth: $2.4 billion

*Public Real Estate Investment Trusts (REITs)*

**America's top REITs, meaning those with the most assets under control, are largely managed by American Jews** and include the following:[52]

- Acadia Realty Trust
  Key Figure: Kenneth Bernstein, CEO

- Boston Properties
  Key Figure: Mortimer Zuckerman, chairman

- CBL & Associates Properties, Inc.
  Key Figure: Charles Lebovitz, chairman
  Key Figure: Stephen Lebovitz, CEO

- Cedar Realty Trust
  Key Figure: Bruce Shanzer, CEO

- Developers Diversified Realty Corporation
  Key Figure: Daniel Hurwitz, CEO

- Equity Residential
  Key Figure: Sam Zell, chairman

- General Growth Properties
  Key Figure: Matthew Bucksbaum, founder

- Glimcher Realty Trust
  Key Figure: Michael Glimcher, CEO

- Kimco Realty Corporation
  Key Figure: Milton Cooper, chairman

- Pennsylvania Real Estate Investment Trust
  Key Figure: Ronald Rubin, chairman

- Ramco-Gershenson Properties Trust
  Key Figure: Stephen Blank, chairman
  Key Figure: Dennis Gershenson, CEO

- Rouse Properties
  Key Figure: Andrew Silberfein, CEO

- Simon Property Group
  Key Figure: David Simon, chairman & CEO

- SL Green Realty Corp
  Key Figure: Stephen L. Green, chairman

- Sun Communities
  Key Figure: Gary Shiffman, chair & CEO

- Tanger Factory Outlet Centers
  Key Figure: Steven Tanger, CEO

- Taubman Centers
  Key Figure: Robert Taubman, CEO

- Vornado Realty Trust
  Key Figure: Steven Roth, chairman

## *Publicly Traded Building Companies*

**Of the ten largest publicly traded building corporations in the United States, no less than four, or forty percent, have Jewish chairmen and/or CEOs.**[53]

- <u>KB Home</u>
  Key Figure: Jeffrey Mezger, CEO

- <u>Lennar Corporation</u>
  Key Figure: Stuart Miller, CEO

- <u>MDC Holdings</u>
  Key Figure: Larry Mizel, chairman and CEO

- <u>Toll Brothers, Inc.</u>
  Key Figure: Robert Toll, chairman

# JEWS IN ENTERTAINMENT

A handful of Americans have questioned Jewish control of Hollywood only to be charged with anti-Semitism and told that such thinking is a slanderous myth. However, simple analysis of the central figures in the movie industry, as well as in television, comedy, and music, clearly illustrates that Jewish-Americans are the ultimate source of power and influence in the entertainment industry. Despite protest from liberal corners, the statistics do not lie and they are overwhelming.

*Jewish Influence in Cinema*

The "Big Six" Film Production and Distribution Companies

**The "Big Six" control the movie industry and, in terms of movie production, each corporation has a parent division and a major studio subsidiary.**[54] **Nine out of twelve of these divisions and subsidiaries, or seventy-five percent, are run by Jews.**

- Comcast
  *Parent Division:*
  NBC Universal
  Key Figure: Steve Burke (not Jewish), CEO

*Major Studio Subsidiary:*
Universal Pictures
Key Figure: Ronald Meyer, president

- News Corporation
  *Parent Division:*
  Fox Entertainment Group
  Key Figure: Jim Gianopolous (not Jewish), chairman &
  CEO

  *M ajor Studio Subsidiary:*
  20th Century Fox
  Key Figure: Jim Gianopolous (not Jewish), chairman &
  CEO

- Sony
  *Parent Division:*
  Sony Pictures Entertainment
  Key Figure: Michael Lynton, chairman & CEO

  *Major Studio Subsidiary:*
  Columbia Pictures
  Key Figure: Doug Belgrad, co-president
  Key Figure: Matt Tolmach, co-president

- Time Warner
  *Parent Division:*
  Warner Brothers Entertainment
  Key Figure: Barry Meyer, chairman

  *Major Studio Subsidiary:*
  Warner Brothers Pictures
  Key Figure: Barry Meyer, chairman

- Viacom
  *Parent Division:*
  Paramount Motion Pictures Group
  Key Figure: Brad Grey, chairman & CEO

  *Major Studio Subsidiary:*
  Paramount Pictures
  Key Figure: Brad Grey, chairman & CEO

- Walt Disney Company
  *Parent Division:*
  Walt Disney Studios
  Key Figure: Alan Horn, chairman

  *Major Studio Subsidiary:*
  Walt Disney Pictures
  Key Figure: Alan Horn, chairman

The Mini-Majors

A mini-major is simply a smaller film production and distribution corporation than those of the "Big Six." However, **the mini-majors listed below** are still influential and **are controlled by some of the most powerful players in Hollywood, all of whom are Jewish**.

- Dream Works: Steven Speilberg, principal
- Dream Works Animation: Jeffrey Katzenberg, CEO
- Lionsgate Films: Patrick Wachsberger and Rob Friedman, co-chairmen
- Relativity Media: Ryan Cavanaugh, CEO
- The Weinstein Company: Bob Weinstein and Harvey Weinstein, co-chairmen
- Metro-Goldwyn-Mayer: Gary Barber, CEO

*Influential Producers*

**Jews dominate the ranks of Hollywood's most powerful movie producers**. The men listed below have access to the money needed to shoot virtually any film they so desire.

- J.J. Abrams – 'Armageddon,' 'Mission: Impossible – Ghost Protocol,' 'Star Trek: Into Darkness'
- Judd Apatow – 'Knocked Up,' 'Superbad,' 'Step Brothers'
- Jerry Bruckheimer – 'Armageddon,' 'Black Hawk Down,' 'Pearl Harbor'
- Ethan Cohen – 'The Big Lebowski,' 'O Brother, Where Art Thou?,' 'No Country For Old Men'
- Joel Cohen – 'Fargo,' 'Burn After Reading,' 'True Grit'
- Robert Evans – 'Chinatown,' 'Urban Cowboy,' 'The Out-of-Towners'
- Joel Silver – 'Lethal Weapon,' 'Die Hard,' 'The Matrix'
- Bob Weinstein – 'Pulp Fiction,' 'The Cider House Rules,' 'Gangs of New York'
- Harvey Weinstein - 'Reservoir Dogs,' 'True Romance,' 'Good Will Hunting'

*Top Directors*

**The top directors in the film industry are mostly Jewish** and include the following:

- Woody Allen – 'Annie Hall,' 'New York Stories,' 'Mighty Aphrodite'
- Milos Forman – 'One Flew Over the Cuckoo's Nest,' 'Amadeus,' 'Man on the Moon'
- George Lucas – 'American Graffiti,' 'Star Wars Episode I: The Phantom Menace,' 'Star Wars Episode II: Attack of the Clones'

- Roman Polanski – 'Rosemary's Baby,' 'Chinatown,' 'The Pianist'
- Sam Raimi – 'A Simple Man,' 'Spider-Man,' 'Spider-Man 2'
- Harold Ramis – 'Caddyshack,' 'Analyze This,' 'Analyze That'
- Rob Reiner – 'Stand by Me,' 'When Harry Met Sally,' 'A Few Good Men'
- Ivan Reitman – 'Meatballs,' 'Stripes,' 'Ghostbusters'
- Steven Soderbergh – 'Erin Brockovich,' 'Traffic,' 'Ocean's Eleven'
- Steven Spielberg – 'Jaws,' 'Indiana Jones and the Temple of Doom,' 'Jurassic Park'
- Oliver Stone – 'Platoon,' 'Wall Street,' 'Born on the Fourth of July'

*Famous Jewish Actors in Cinema*

**The following list is but a mere sampling of famous Jewish actors**, yet is so long and includes so many A-list celebrities that one would think only Jews are admitted to the Screen Actors Guild:

- F. Murray Abraham – 'Scarface,' 'Amadeus'
- Alan Arkin – 'The Heart is a Lonely Hunter,' 'Argo'
- David Arquette – 'Scream,' 'Scream 2'
- Patricia Arquette – 'True Romance,' 'Bringing Out the Dead'
- Rosanna Arquette – 'Pulp Fiction,' 'The Whole Nine Yards'
- Barbara Bach – 'The Spy Who Loved Me,' 'Force 10 from Navarone'
- Elizabeth Banks – 'The Forty-Year-Old Virgin,' 'Role Models'
- Ellen Barkin – 'Ocean's Thirteen,' 'Brooklyn's Finest'
- Jay Baruchel – 'Million Dollar Baby,' 'Knocked Up'
- Randall Batinkoff – 'School Ties,' 'Higher Learning'
- Peter Berg – 'Cop Land,' 'Collateral'

- Jack Black – 'Shallow Hal,' 'School of Rock'
- Selma Blair – 'Legally Blonde,' 'The Sweetest Thing'
- Orlando Bloom – 'The Lord of the Rings,' 'Pirates of the Caribbean'
- Matthew Broderick – 'Ferris Bueller's Day Off,' 'Glory'
- Adrien Brody – 'Summer of Sam,' 'The Pianist'
- Albert Brooks – 'The Scout,' 'The In-Laws'
- James Caan – 'The Godfather,' 'Mickey Blue Eyes'
- Neve Campbell – 'Scream,' 'Wild Things'
- Dyan Cannon – 'Heaven Can Wait,' 'She's Having a Baby'
- Lizzy Caplan – 'Mean Girls,' 'My Best Friend's Girl'
- Kate Capshaw – 'Indiana Jones and the Temple of Doom,' 'Black Rain'
- Phoebe Cates – 'Fast Times at Ridgemont High,' 'Gremlins'
- Josh Charles – 'Dead Poets Society,' 'Four Brothers'
- Sacha Baron Cohen – 'Borat,' 'The Dictator'
- Jennifer Connelly – 'Requiem for a Dream,' 'A Beautiful Mind'
- Peter Coyote – 'Femme Fatale,' 'A Walk to Remember'
- Billy Crystal – 'Analyze This,' 'Analyze That'
- Jamie Lee Curtis – 'True Lies,' 'Freaky Friday'
- Daniel Day-Lewis – 'The Last of the Mohicans,' 'There Will Be Blood'
- Stephen Dorff – 'Blade,' 'Cold Creek Manor'
- Michael Douglass – 'Wall Street,' 'A Perfect Murder'
- Robert Downey, Jr. – 'Iron Man,' 'Sherlock Holmes'
- Richard Dreyfuss – 'Close Encounters of the Third Kind,' 'Mr. Holland's Opus'
- Jesse Eisenberg – 'Zombieland,' 'The Social Network'
- Zac Efron – '17 Again,' 'Charlie St. Cloud'
- Jon Favreau – 'The Break-Up,' 'Couples Retreat'
- Corey Feldman – 'The Goonies,' 'Stand By Me'
- Carrie Fisher – 'Star Wars,' 'The 'Burbs'
- Isla Fisher – 'Wedding Crashers,' 'The Lookout'
- Harrison Ford – 'Star Wars,' 'Raiders of the Lost Ark'

- Ben Foster – 'Alpha Dog,' 'The Messenger'
- James Franco – 'Pineapple Express,' 'Oz the Great and Powerful'
- Gina Gershon – 'Cocktail,' 'Show Girls'
- Scott Glenn – 'Training Day,' 'The Bourne Ultimatum'
- Jeff Goldblum – 'Jurassic Park,' 'Independence Day'
- Adam Golderg – 'A Beautiful Mind,' 'The Salton Sea'
- Joseph Gordon-Levitt – 'Angels in the Outfield,' '10 Things I Hate About You'
- Elliot Gould – 'Ocean's Eleven,' 'Ocean's Twelve'
- Seth Green – 'Austin Powers: International Man of Mystery,' 'The Italian Job'
- Brian Greenberg – 'Bride Wars,' 'Friends with Benefits'
- Jennifer Grey – 'Ferris Bueller's Day Off,' 'Dirty Dancing'
- Steve Guttenberg – 'Police Academy,' 'Three Men and a Baby'
- Jake Gyllenhaal – 'Jarhead,' 'Love and Other Drugs'
- Maggie Gyllenhaal – 'World Trade Center,' 'The Dark Knight'
- Daryl Hannah – 'Steel Magnolias,' 'Kill Bill'
- Cole Hauser – 'Paparazzi,' 'The Family That Preys'
- Goldie Hawn – 'Overboard,' 'The First Wives Club'
- Dan Hedaya – 'Rookie of the Year,' 'Clueless'
- Barbara Hershey – 'Hoosiers,' 'Beaches'
- Jonah Hill – 'Superbad,' 'Moneyball'
- Emile Hirsch – 'The Girl Next Door,' 'Into the Wild'
- Dustin Hoffman – 'Rain Man,' 'Meet the Fockers'
- Kate Hudson – 'Almost Famous,' 'How to Lose a Guy in 10 Days'
- Scarlett Johansson – 'The Horse Whisperer,' 'Girl with a Pearl Earring'
- Carol Kane – 'Annie Hall,' 'When a Stranger Calls'
- Ben Kingsley – 'Gandhi,' 'Schindler's List'
- Mia Kirshner – 'Party Monster,' 'The Black Dahlia'
- Kevin Kline – 'In & Out,' 'Life as a House'

- Yaphet Kotto – 'Live and Let Die,' 'Midnight Run'
- Mila Kunis – 'Forgetting Sarah Marshall,' 'Black Swan'
- Martin Landau – 'Rounders,' 'Ready to Rumble'
- Shia Lebeouf – 'Disturbia,' 'Transformers'
- Jennifer Jason Leigh – 'Single White Female,' 'The Hudsucker Proxy'
- Eugene Levy – 'American Pie,' 'American Reunion'
- Jonathan Lipnicki – 'Jerry Maguire,' 'Stuart Little'
- Jon Lovitz – '3000 Miles to Graceland,' 'Rat Race'
- Natasha Lyonne – 'American Pie,' 'Blade: Trinity'
- Ali MacGraw – 'Love Story,' 'The Getaway'
- Larry Miller – 'A Guy Thing,' 'A Mighty Wind'
- Christopher Mintz-Plasse – 'Superbad,' 'Role Models'
- Rick Moranis – 'Honey, I Shrunk The Kids,' 'My Blue Heaven'
- Judd Nelson – 'The Breakfast Club,' 'St. Elmo's Fire'
- Tim Blake Nelson – 'O Brother, Where Art Though?,' 'Minority Report'
- Gwyneth Paltrow – 'Shakespeare in Love,' 'The Talented Mr. Ripley'
- David Paymer – 'The American President,' 'State and Main'
- Amanda Peet – 'The Whole Nine Yards,' 'The Whole Ten Yards'
- Sean Penn – 'Mystic River,' 'Milk'
- Joaquin Phoenix – 'Gladiator,' 'Walk the Line'
- Sydney Pollack – 'Eyes Wide Shut,' 'Changing Lanes'
- Kevin Pollak – 'A Few Good Men,' 'Casino'
- Natalie Portman – 'Brothers,' 'Black Swan'
- Freddie Prinze, Jr. – 'I Know What You Did Last Summer,' 'She's All That'
- Daniel Radcliffe – 'The Tailor of Panama,' 'Harry Potter and the Philosopher's Stone'
- Michael Rappaport – 'Beautiful Girls,' 'Men of Honor'
- Nikki Reed – 'Lords of Dogtown,' 'Twilight'

- Seth Rogen – 'Funny People,' 'The Green Hornet'
- Emmy Rossum – 'The Phantom of the Opera,' 'Poseidon'
- Paul Rudd – 'Wanderlust,' 'This is 40'
- Wynona Ryder – 'Heathers,' 'Mr. Deeds'
- Adam Sandler – 'Billy Madison,' 'Happy Gilmore'
- Rob Schneider – 'Deuce Bigalow: Male Gigolo,' 'The Hot Chick'
- Liev Schreiber – 'The Sum of All Fears,' 'Love in the Time of Cholera'
- Steven Seagal – 'Above the Law,' 'Under Siege'
- Jane Seymour – 'Live and Let Die,' 'East of Eden'
- Wallace Shawn – 'My Dinner with Andre,' 'The Princess Bride'
- Ally Sheedy – 'The Breakfast Club,' 'St. Elmo's Fire'
- Pauly Shore – 'Son in Law,' 'In the Army Now'
- Jonathan Silverman – 'Weekend at Bernie's,' 'Weekend at Bernie's 2'
- Sarah Silverman – 'School for Scoundrels,' 'Funny People'
- Alicia Silverstone – 'Clueless,' 'Excess Baggage'
- Marla Sokoloff – 'Whatever it Takes,' 'Sugar & Spice'
- Daniel Stern – 'Home Alone,' 'Home Alone 2'
- Ben Stiller – 'Meet the Parents,' 'Night at the Museum'
- Eddie Kaye Thomas – 'American Pie,' 'Harold & Kumar Go to White Castle'
- Rachel Weisz – 'Enemy at the Gates,' 'The Constant Gardener'
- Debra Winger – 'An Officer and a Gentleman,' 'Terms of Endearment'
- Evan Rachel Wood – 'Thirteen,' 'The Wrestler'

### Jewish Influence in Television

We have already noted that **all four of the major television networks, ABC, CBS, FOX, and NBC, have Jewish chairmen**

**and CEOs**, but it is important to remember that the **Public Broadcasting Service (PBS) and hundreds of cable television channels are run by Jewish-Americans as well.** Therefore, these individuals have the power to control the content of the programming that comes into the homes of hundreds of millions of Americans on a daily basis.

## Network Television

- American Broadcasting Corporation (ABC)
  Owned by Walt Disney Company
  Key Figure: Bob Iger, chairman & CEO

- Columbia Broadcasting System (CBS)
  Owned by CBS Corporation
  Key Figure: Sumner Redstone, chairman
  Key Figure: Leslie Moonves, CEO

- Fox Broadcasting Company (FOX)
  Owned by News Corporation
  Key Figure: Rupert Murdoch, chairman & CEO

- National Broadcasting Corporation (NBC)
  Owned by Comcast Corporation
  Key Figure: Brian Roberts, chairman & CEO

- Public Broadcasting Service (PBS)
  Key Figure: Paula Kerger, CEO

## Cable Networks

Jewish influence in cable television is no less apparent than in network television. **The following companies, which are all headed by Jews, combine to own hundreds of cable television channels:**

- AMC Networks
  Key Figure: Joshua Sapan, CEO
  Top Channels: American Movie Channel (AMC), Independent Film Channel (IFC), Sundance Channel, and WeTV

- Bloomberg LP
  Key Figure: Michael Bloomberg, owner
  Top Channel: Bloomberg TV

- Discovery Communications
  Key Figure: David Zaslav, CEO
  Top Channels: Animal Planet, Discovery Channel, The Learning Channel (TLC), Military Channel, and the Oprah Winfrey Network (OWN; fifty percent stake)

- InterActiveCorp
  Key Figure: Barry Diller, chairman
  Top Channel: Home Shopping Network

- News Corporation
  Key Figure: Rupert Murdoch, owner
  Top Channels: Fuel TV, FX Channel, National Geographic Channel, and Speed TV

- Showtime Networks
  Key Figure: Matthew Blank, chairman & CEO
  Top Channels: Flix Channel, The Movie Channel (TMC), Showtime Channels, and Smithsonian Channel

- Viacom Media Networks
  Key Figure: Doug Herzog, president
  Top Channels: Comedy Central, Country Music Television (CMT), Music Television (MTV), Nickelodeon Channel, Palladia Channel, Spike TV, TV Land, and VH1

- <u>Walt Disney Company</u>
  Key Figure: Bog Iger, chairman & CEO
  Top Channels: ESPN, ESPN2, and ESPN Classic

*Famous Jewish Actors on Television*

**With thousands of actors appearing on the hundreds of channels in existence, it is impossible to quantify the Jewish presence on television. It can be concluded, however, that Jews comprise an inordinately high percentage of the most famous and influential actors on television.**

- Paula Abdul – 'American Idol'
- Jason Alexander – 'Seinfeld'
- Shiri Appleby – 'Roswell'
- Adam Arkin – 'Chicago Hope'
- Tom Arnold – 'Roseanne'
- Bea Arthur – 'Golden Girls'
- Ed Asner – 'The Mary Tyler Moore Show'
- Hank Azaria – 'The Simpsons'
- Roseanne Barr – 'Roseanne'
- Richard Belzer – 'Law & Order: SVU'
- Elizabeth Berkeley – 'Saved by the Bell'
- Corbin Bernsen – 'L.A. Law'
- Mayim Bialik – 'Blossom'
- Rachel Bilson – 'The O.C.'
- Michael Ian Black – 'Ed'
- Yasmine Bleeth – 'Baywatch'
- Peter Bogdanovich – 'The Sopranos'
- Lisa Bonet – 'The Cosby Show'
- Zach Braff – 'Scrubs'
- Adam Brody – 'The O.C.'
- Brooke Burke – 'Wild On!'
- Amanda Bynes – 'What I Like About You'
- Scott Caan – 'Hawaii Five-O'

- Gabrielle Carteris – 'Beverly Hills 90210'
- Stockard Channing – 'The West Wing'
- David Charvet – 'Baywatch'
- Joan Collins – 'Dynasty'
- Paulo Costanzo – 'Royal Pains'
- Mark Cuban – 'Shark Tank'
- Eric Dane – 'Grey's Anatomy'
- Larry David – 'Curb Your Enthusiasm'
- Dustin Diamond – 'Saved by the Bell'
- Scott Disick – 'Keeping Up with the Kardashians'
- Rachel Dratch – 'Saturday Night Live'
- Fran Drescher – 'The Nanny'
- David Duchovny – 'The X-Files'
- Lisa Edelstein – 'House'
- Mark Feuerstein – 'Royal Pains'
- Bethenny Frankel – 'The Real Housewives of New York City'
- Judah Friedlander – '30 Rock'
- Jeff Garlin – 'Curb Your Enthusiasm'
- Brad Garrett – 'Everybody Loves Raymond'
- Sarah Michelle Gellar – 'Buffy the Vampire Slayer'
- Jami Gertz – 'Still Standing'
- Kathie Lee Gifford – 'Regis and Kathie Lee'
- Jonathan Gilbert – 'Little House on the Prairie'
- Melissa Gilbert – 'Little House on the Prairie'
- Sara Gilbert - 'Roseanne'
- Whoppi Goldberg – 'The View'
- Chelsea Handler – 'Chelsea Lately'
- Alyson Hannigan – 'Buffy the Vampire Slayer'
- Simon Helberg – 'Big Bang Theory'
- Judd Hirsch – 'Taxi'
- Oliver Hudson – 'Rules of Engagement'
- Helen Hunt – 'Mad About You'
- Rashida Jones – 'Parks and Recreation'
- Gabe Kaplan – 'Welcome Back, Kotter'

- Richard Kind – 'Spin City'
- Lisa Kudrow – 'Friends'
- Ricki Lake – 'The Ricki Lake Show'
- Piper Laurie – 'Twin Peaks'
- Judith Light – 'Who's the Boss?'
- Julia Louis-Dreyfuss – 'Seinfeld'
- Bill Maher – 'Real Time with Bill Maher'
- Leonard Maltin – 'Entertainment Tonight'
- Howie Mandel – 'Deal or No Deal'
- Camryn Manheim – 'The Practice'
- Julianna Margulies – 'The Good Wife'
- Deborah Messing – 'Will and Grace'
- Lorne Michaels – 'Saturday Night Live'
- Donny Most – 'Happy Days'
- Bebe Neuwirth – 'Cheers'
- Leonard Nimoy – 'Star Trek'
- Bill Nye – 'Bill Nye the Science Guy'
- Jerry Orbach – 'Law & Order'
- Sharon Osbourne – 'The Osbournes'
- Mandy Pantinkin – 'Criminal Minds'
- Sarah Jessica Parker – 'Sex and the City'
- Rhea Perlman – 'Cheers'
- Ron Perlman – 'Sons of Anarchy'
- Bronson Pinchot – 'Perfect Strangers'
- Jeremy Piven – 'Entourage'
- Tracy Pollan – 'Family Ties'
- Maury Povich – 'The Maury Povich Show'
- Josh Radnor – 'How I Met Your Mother'
- Sally Jessy Raphael – 'Sally'
- Paul Reiser – 'Mad About You'
- Leah Remini – 'The King of Queens'
- Paul Reubens – 'The Pee Wee Herman Show'
- Simon Rex – 'What I Like About You'
- Geraldo Rivera – 'Geraldo'
- Joan Rivers – 'Fashion Police'

- Doris Roberts – 'Everybody Loves Raymond'
- Michael Rosenbaum – 'Smallville'
- Saul Rubinek – 'Frasier'
- Katey Sagal – 'Married with Children'
- Bob Saget – 'Full House'
- Andy Samberg – 'Saturday Night Live'
- Ben Savage – 'Boy Meets World'
- Fred Savage – 'The Wonder Years'
- Jason Schwartzman – 'Bored to Death'
- David Schwimmer – 'Friends'
- Kyra Sedgwick – 'The Closer'
- Jason Segel – 'How I Met Your Mother'
- Jerry Seinfeld – 'Seinfeld'
- Paul Shaffer – 'Late Show with David Letterman'
- Gary Shandling – 'The Gary Shandling Show'
- William Shatner – 'Star Trek'
- Judy Sheindlin – 'Judge Judy'
- Jamie-Lynn Sigler – 'The Sopranos'
- Tori Spelling – 'Beverly Hills 90210'
- Jordana Spiro – 'My Boys'
- Jerry Springer – 'The Jerry Springer Show'
- Patti Stanger – 'The Millionaire Matchmaker'
- Ben Stein – 'Win Ben Stein's Money'
- Jon Stewart – 'The Daily Show'
- Jerry Stiller – 'The King of Queens'
- Michelle Trachtenberg – 'Buffy the Vampire Slayer'
- Michael Vartan – 'Alias'
- Joseph Wapner – 'The People's Court'
- Steven Weber – 'Wings'
- Henry Winkler – 'Happy Days'
- Mare Winningham – 'Law & Order: SVU'
- Scott Wolf – 'Party of Five'
- Robert Wuhl – 'Arliss'
- Noah Wyle – 'ER'
- Ian Ziering – 'Beverly Hills 90210'

## *Jewish Influence in Comedy*

From a philosophical viewpoint, stand-up comedy is actually a serious critique of our society – under the guise of humor, co-medians are free to promulgate their own personal opinions on a range of topics. **With so many of the most famous American comedians being Jewish, our society is therefore being analyzed and judged by a small group of people from a similar back-ground, all viewing the people and ideas they mock through the same colored lens.**

*Famous Jewish Comedians*

- Dave Attell
- Sandra Bernhard
- Lewis Black
- Michael Ian Black
- Albert Brooks
- Mel Brooks
- Andrew Dice Clay
- Billy Crystal
- Judy Gold
- Gilbert Gottfried
- Robert Klein
- Jerry Lewis
- Richard Lewis
- Jackie Mason
- Don Rickels
- Jeffrey Ross
- Rita Rudner
- Bob Saget
- Adam Sandler
- Robert Schimmel
- Amy Schumer

- Jerry Seinfeld
- Gary Shandling
- Sarah Silverman
- Jason Sklar
- Randy Sklar
- Jon Stewart
- Jerry Stiller
- Steven Wright

### *Jewish Influence in Music*

Over the past several years, a frenetic pace of mergers and acquisitions has resulted in the consolidation of the music industry into just three major recording companies, known as the "Big Three."[55] Accordingly, these three companies now have nearly complete control over the artists that are signed to recording deals and the musical content that reaches the end listener. **All of the "Big Three" recording companies, or one hundred percent, are headed by American Jews.**

The "Big Three" Recording Companies

- Sony Music Entertainment
  Key Figure: Doug Morris, chairman & CEO
  –Labels: Columbia Records, Epic Records, RCA Records

- Universal Music Group
  Key Figure: Zach Horowitz, president
  –Labels: Capitol Records, Def Jam Records, Geffen Records, Interscope Records, Island Records, Virgin Records

- Warner Music Group
  Key Figure: Stephen Cooper, CEO
  –Labels: Atlantic Records, Elektra Records, EMI Records

*Jewish Performers and Singers*

**As with movies, television, and comedy, Jews are grossly overrepresented in the American music industry in relation to their percentage of the population.**

- Paula Abdul
- Burt Bacarach
- Marty Balin
- Pat Benetar
- Jay Black
- Michael Bolton
- Aaron Carter
- Nick Carter
- Harry Connick, Jr.
- Chris Cornell
- Taylor Dane
- Craig David
- Michael "Mike-D" Diamond
- Neil Diamond
- Drake
- Adam Duritz
- Bob Dylan
- Jakob Dylan
- Donald Fagen
- Marianne Faithfull
- Perry Farrell
- Kenny G
- Art Garfunkel
- Leslie Gore
- Edyie Gorme
- Josh Groban
- Arlo Guthrie
- Beck Hansen
- Susanna Hoffs

- Adam "Ad-Rock" Horovitz
- Enrique Iglesias
- Julio Iglesias
- Billy Joel
- Carole King
- Lenny Kravitz
- Robbie Krieger
- Adam Lambert
- K.D. Lang
- Steve Lawrence
- Adam Levine
- Lisa Loeb
- Courtney Love
- Melissa Manchester
- Barry Manilow
- Manfred Mann
- Richard Marx
- John Mayer
- George Michael
- Bette Midler
- Randy Newman
- Ric Ocasek
- Steven Page
- Pink
- Joey Ramone
- Lou Reed
- Robbie Robertson
- Chris Robinson
- Rich Robinson
- Gavin Rossdale
- David Lee Roth
- Neil Sedaka
- Gene Simmons
- Carly Simon
- Paul Simon

- Slash
- Dee Snider
- Phil Spector
- Regina Spektor
- Paul Stanley
- Barbara Streisand
- James Taylor
- Max Weinberg
- Peter Yarrow

# JEWS IN CULTURE

When a handful of largely like-minded people control the culture of a country as large as the United States of America, that oligarchy has the ability to determine exactly that which passes as "civilized" and "refined" for hundreds of millions of people. "High-culture" in America includes such pursuits as art, classical music, theater, fashion, and wine. Operating entirely out of New York City (save for wine), the self-proclaimed cultural center of the world and home to the second largest enclave of Jews on earth, these five endeavors have become the exclusive domain of a scant two percent of the population.

*Jewish Influence in the New York City Art Scene*

**The world of art in New York City is the world of art in America, which is to say that art anywhere else in the United States is entirely overlooked and, therefore, does not matter.** A recent article listing the most powerful and influential figures in the New York City art scene was rife with Jewish surnames, almost to the complete exclusion of everyone else.[56] And according to the most recent report from the National Endowment for the Arts, fifty-one million people visit art museums and galleries each year, making this a multi-billion dollar industry.[57]

## Jewish Benefactors & Collectors

–These are the figures that patronize the New York City art scene with their wealth, buying expensive works for their private collections and donating to the foundations and museums that meet with their approbation.

- Phillip Aarons – A prominent figure in New York City real estate, Aarons is a serious collector of modern art and patron of artists like Tom Sachs
- Melva Bucksbaum – From a wealthy real estate family, Bucksbaum is a collector, patroness, and serves on the board of the Museum of Modern Art
- Glenn Furhman – An avid collector of contemporary art, Fuhrman has built his personal collection using the millions of dollars he has made through his private equity group, MSD Capital.
- Brooke Garber-Neidich – Daughter of a famous Chicago jeweler, Garber-Neidich has an extensive private collection and also serves on the board of the Whitney Museum of American Art
- Ronald Lauder – Worth an estimated $3.4 billion, Lauder is an heir to the Estee Lauder cosmetics fortune and a premier collector of art
- Adam Lindemann – A player in the lucrative world of private equity, Lindemann has amassed a sizeable collection of contemporary art
- Jose Mugrabi – A Syrian Jew who built a fortune in textiles, Mugrabi now owns the world's largest collection of Andy Warhol paintings
- Beth Rudin – From a prominent New York City real estate family, Rudin is a major collector and patroness of Jewish artists such as Cindy Sherman and Nan Goldin

Jewish Art Dealers & Gallery Owners

–These are the figures that own and operate the galleries in which works are displayed for sale to the general public. They have the power to pick and choose the types of art showcased in their galleries and they also have a say in which artists become prominent within the ranks of their closely guarded community.

- Amalia Dayan – Owner of Luxembourg & Dayan, an elite gallery on the Upper East Side of Manhattan
- Barbara Gladstone – Owner of the Gladstone Gallery in Manhattan, exhibits work by the likes of Matthew Barney and Sarah Lucas
- Marc Glimcher – Owner of Pace Gallery, which has four locations in Manhattan
- Jeanne Greenberg-Rohatyn – Owner of Salon 94, a franchise of galleries located across Manhattan
- Casey Kaplan – Owner of the Casey Kaplan Gallery in New York City's Chelsea neighborhood, features artists such as Matthew Brannon and Simon Starling
- Dominique Levy – Co-owns L&M Arts, one of New York City's most exclusive galleries, with Robert Mnuchin
- Joel Mesler – Owner of Untitled Gallery on the Lower East Side of Manhattan
- Robert Mnuchin – With Dominique Levy, the former Goldman Sachs executive owns the L&M Arts gallery, which caters to the likes of hedge fund billionaire Steve Cohen

Jewish Administrators & Curators

–These are the figures that run New York City's preeminent art museums. They include museum administrators and curators, the people working behind the scenes and in front of the exhibits.

- RoseLee Goldberg – Founding director and curator of the Performa Institute, which explores the role of live art in the twentieth century and the new millennium
- Kathy Halbreich – Associate director of the Museum of Modern Art, oversees both fundraising and exhibitions
- Kate Levin – Commissioner of the New York City Department of Cultural Affairs, which dispenses $27 million of taxpayer money to art organizations across the five boroughs each year[58]
- Tobias Meyer – Serves as Worldwide Head of Contemporary Art for Sotheby's from its New York City headquarters
- Lisa Phillips – Director of the New Museum of Contemporary Art since 1999
- Jay Saners – Curator of the Whitney Museum of American Art
- Vito Schnabel – Freelance curator based in Manhattan's West Village section, has worked for museums around the world
- Amanda Sharp – Stages the annual Frieze Art Fair that is attended by New York City's art world elite
- Nancy Spector – Deputy director and chief curator of the Guggenheim Museum
- Joel Wachs – President of the Andy Warhol Foundation for the Visual Arts since 2001
- Adam Weinberg – Director of the Whitney Museum of American Art since 2003

Jewish Artists

–These are the figures that produce the actual works of art and vie for a place in New York City's museums and galleries.

- Ross Bleckner – Focuses on the topics of change and loss, has been displayed in the Guggenheim Museum and the Museum of Modern Art

- Alex Katz – Pop artist, work routinely displayed at the Whitney Museum of Modern Art
- Julian Schnabel – Famous for his plate paintings, work is often exhibited by the Pace Gallery
- Cindy Sherman – Works sells for top-dollar at auction, has been exhibited by the Museum of Modern Art
- Amy Sillman – Focuses on abstract art, work can often be viewed at the Museum of Modern Art

Jewish Critics & Journalists

–These are the figures that cover New York City's art scene for the area's major newspapers and magazines, of which there are a multitude.

- Knight Landesman – Publisher of *ArtForum* magazine, which is headquartered in Manhattan
- Jerry Saltz – Senior art critic for *New York* magazine
- Amanda Sharp – Co-founder of *Frieze*, an influential contemporary art magazine
- Linda Yablonsky – Chief *New York Times* art critic

*Jews in Classical Music*

While almost none of classical music's legendary composers from the seventeenth century to the nineteenth century were Jewish (Gustav Mahler and Felix Mendelsohn representing prominent exceptions), classical music in America is now dominated by Jews.

**Classical music in America is now defined by the "Big Five" symphony orchestras**, each located in a major eastern or mid-western city.[59] And **no less than two of the five administrators of the "Big Five," or forty percent, are Jewish (among recent conductors of the "Big Five," Jews represent an even greater percentage)**. According to the most recent report from the National Endowment for the

Arts, twenty-one million people attend classical music performances each year, making this a multi-billion dollar industry.

## The "Big Five" Symphony Orchestras

- Boston Symphony Orchestra
  Administrator: Boston Symphony Orchestra
  Key Figure: Julian Cohen, managing director

  *Recent Jewish Conductors:*

  James Levine
  William Steinberg
  Erich Leinsdorf

- Chicago Symphony Orchestra
  Administrator: Chicago Symphony Orchestra
  Key Figure: William Osborn (not Jewish), chairman

  *Recent Jewish Conductors:*

  Daniel Barenboim
  Georg Solti
  Irwin Hoffman
  Fritz Reiner

- Cleveland Orchestra
  Administrator: Cleveland Orchestra
  Key Figure: Gary Hanson (religion: unknown), executive director

  *Recent Jewish Conductors:*

  Lorin Maazel
  George Szell

Erich Leinsdorf

- New York Philharmonic
  Administrator: Philharmonic-Symphony Society of New York
  Key Figure: Gary Parr, chairman

*Recent Jewish Conductors:*

Alan Gilbert
Lorin Maazel
Leonard Bernstein

- Philadelphia Orchestra
  Administrator: Philadelphia Orchestra
  Key Figure: Richard Worley (religion: unknown), chairman

*Recent Jewish Conductors:*

Eugene Ormandy

## Jews in Theater

As with visual art, important stage theater in the United States is restricted to a single locale: New York City. If a performance is not taking place on Broadway, then it is not considered to be important. And **Broadway is absolutely dominated by Jewish-Americans.**

Broadway is technically defined as the forty Manhattan theaters offering seating for five hundred or more people.[60] In 2012, over twelve million people attended Broadway shows with ticket sales worth an estimated $1 billion, which means that Broadway is big business.[61]

## Jewish Theater Ownership

**–No less than thirty-one of Broadway's forty theaters, or seventy-eight percent, are owned and operated by Jews:**

- Shubert Organization
  Owns seventeen Broadway theaters
  Key Figure: Robert Wankel, president and co-CEO

- Nederlander Organization
  Owns nine Broadway theaters
  Key Figure: James Nederlander, president

- Jujamcyn Theaters
  Owns five Broadway theaters
  Key Figure: Jordan Roth, owner

*Famous Jewish Producers*

- Bernard Gersten – *Six Degrees of Separation, Spinning Into Butter*
- Nicholas Hytner – *Miss Saigon, The History Boys*
- Paul Libin – *The Iceman Cometh, Tricks of the Trade*
- Scott Rudin – *Passion, Fences*
- David Stone – *Man of La Mancha, Wicked*
- Barry Weisler – *My Fair Lady, Chicago*

*Famous Jewish Composers, Lyricists, and Writers*

- Alan Menken – Musical composer, *The Little Mermaid, Newsies*
- Stephen Schwartz – Lyricist, *Pippin, Wicked*
- Neil Simon – Playwright, *Barefoot in the Park, The Odd Couple*
- Stephen Sondheim – Musical composer, *Follies, Sweeney Todd*

*Other Important Jewish Figures on Broadway*

- Ted Chapin – Chairman of the American Theater Wing and president of the Rodgers & Hammerstein Organization
- Rocco Landesman – Chairman of National Endowment for the Arts, an independent agency of the federal government
- Bernie Telsey – The most powerful casting director on Broadway

## Jews in the Fashion Industry

**Nearly all of America's most famous and influential fashion designers are Jews based in New York City**, and reaching the pinnacle of fashion in the United States brings with it an obscene amount of power and wealth. Many of the individuals listed below are billionaires and the rest are nearly so, which is not surprising given that a 2011 report indicated that the fashion industry in the United States is worth an estimated $199 billion.[62] But the power of a famous fashion designer stretches beyond financial gain. These men and women influence the manner in which Americans dress, which has become scandalously liberal in recent years, and they can also impact the concept of body image among young women.

*Famous Jewish Fashion Designers*

- Kenneth Cole
- Marc Ecko
- Marc Jacobs
- Donna Karan
- Calvin Klein
- Michael Kors
- Ralph Lauren
- Isaac Mizrahi
- Zac Posen

- Diane Von Furstenberg
- Rachel Zoe

*Jewish Influence in Wine*

**While the wine industry in America has only been prominent since the early 1970s, it is already massively important and Jewish control over the industry is ever-increasing.** In fact, the United States is the world's largest market for wine consumption and in 2010 the industry was worth approximately $40 billion.[63] A recent list of the most important figures in wine, including distributors, vintners, and writers, included an excessive number of Jewish names.[64]

Jewish Importers/Distributors
–The top figures on the business side of the industry are predominantly Jewish.

- Wayne Chaplin – President of Southern Wine & Spirits, the largest distributor in America
- Robert Sands – President & CEO of Constellation Brands, the world's largest wine company
- Eric Solomon – President of European Cellars, the leading American importer of high-end wine
- Jon Rimmerman – Founder of Garagiste, the leading online seller of wine in the United States

Jewish Vintners
–While not historically significant, the number of Jewish growers and the acreage under their collective cultivation is rising by the year.

- Kent Rosenblum – Founder of Rosenblum Cellars, a California producer of Zinfandel
- Jerry Lohr – Owner of J. Lohr Vineyards & Wines, a California producer of Cabernet Sauvignon with thirty-seven hundred acres under cultivation

- Stephen Miller – Owner of Bien Nacido Vineyards, a California producer of Chardonnay and Pinot Noir with eight hundred acres under cultivation

## Other Important Jewish Figures in Wine

- Eric Levine – Founder of Cellar Tracker (www.cellartracker. com), a "leading cellar management tool with hundreds of thousands of collectors tracking bottles numbering in the tens of millions"[65]
- Alyssa Rapp – Founder of Bottlenotes (www.bottlenotes. com), a wine community website where millions exchange reviews and give recommendations

## Jewish Wine Writers

- Robert Parker – Publisher of *Wine Advocate* newsletter, arguably the most influential voice in the industry
- Marvin Shanken – Publisher of *Wine Spectator*, the most popular magazine covering the industry
- Matt Kramer – Most influential writer for *Wine Spectator* magazine
- Evan Goldstein – Writer, president of Full Circle Wine Solutions, "a global wine education firm"[66]

## Jewish Wine Critics

- Eric Asimov – Chief wine critic for the *New York Times*
- Tyler Colman – The single-most influential blogger in the industry, writes under the pseudonym "Dr. Vino"
- Alice Feiring – Has covered wine for nearly every major newspaper in America, publishes "The Feiring Line" wine blog

# JEWS IN SPORTS

Americans are a sports-obsessed people, perhaps outdone in their fervor only by Europe's soccer hooligans. According to a 2012 report, the sports industry in America is worth an estimated $414 billion, an impressive three percent of the nation's gross domestic product.[67] And while Jews likely comprise less than one percent of all professional athletes, they dominate the business side of America's four major sports: baseball, basketball, football, and hockey.

*League Commissioners*

**–Three of the four heads of America's major sports associations, or seventy-five percent, are Jewish.**

- Major League Baseball (MLB): Bud Selig, appointed in 1992
- National Basketball Association (NBA): David Stern, appointed in 1984
- National Football League (NFL): Roger Goodell (not Jewish), appointed in 2006
- National Hockey League (NHL): Gary Bettman, appointed in 1993

*Franchise Owners*

**–Across America's four major sports, Jews own no less than thirty-seven percent of all franchises.**

Major League Baseball (MLB)
**–No less than ten of thirty MLB franchises, or thirty-three percent, are owned or controlled by Jews**

- Tampa Bay Rays – Stuart Sternberg
- Toronto Blue Jays – Owned by Rogers Communications: Alan Horn, chairman
- Chicago White Sox – Jerry Reinsdorf
- Kansas City Royals – David Glass
- Oakland Athletics – Lewis Wolff
- Miami Marlins – Jeffrey Loria
- New York Mets – Fred Wilpon
- Washington Nationals – Ted Lerner
- Los Angeles Dodgers – Owned by Guggenheim Baseball Management: Alan Schwartz, chairman
- San Francisco Giants – Owned by San Francisco Baseball Associates LP: Laurence Baer, CEO

National Basketball Association (NBA)
**–No less than fourteen of thirty NBA franchises, or forty-seven percent, are owned or controlled by Jews**

- Dallas Mavericks – Mark Cuban
- Boston Celtics – Wycliffe Grousbeck
- Philadelphia 76ers – Joshua Harris
- Toronto Raptors – Owned by Maple Leaf Sports & Entertainment: Lawrence Tanenbaum, chairman
- Chicago Bulls – Jerry Reinsdorf
- Cleveland Cavaliers – Daniel Gilbert
- Indiana Pacers – Herbert Simon

- Milwaukee Bucks – Herb Kohl
- Atlanta Hawks – Bruce Levenson and Michael Gearon, Jr., majority owners
- Miami Heat – Micky Arison
- Golden State Warriors – Peter Guber, co-owner
- Los Angeles Clippers – Donald Sterling
- Phoenix Suns – Robert Sarver
- Houston Rockets – Leslie Alexander

National Football League (NFL)
**–No less than eleven of thirty-two NFL franchises, or thirty-four percent, are owned by Jews**

- Miami Dolphins – Stephen Ross
- New England Patriots – Robert Kraft
- Cincinnati Bengals – Michael Brown
- Indianapolis Colts – James Irsay
- Oakland Raiders – Mark Davis
- New York Giants – Steve Tisch, co-owner
- Philadelphia Eagles – Jeffrey Lurie
- Washington Redskins – Daniel Snyder
- Minnesota Vikings – Zygi Wilf
- Atlanta Falcons – Arthur Blank
- Tampa Bay Buccaneers – Malcolm Glazer

National Hockey League
**–No less than ten of thirty NHL franchises, or thirty-three percent, are owned or controlled by Jews**

- Philadelphia Flyers – Owned by Comcast Spectacor: Edward Snider, chairman
- Boston Bruin – Jeremy Jacobs
- Toronto Maple Leafs – Owned by Maple Leaf Sports & Entertainment: Larry Tanenbaum, chairman

- Florida Panthers – Owned by Sunrise Sports and Entertainment: Cliff Viner, chairman
- Tampa Bay Lightning – Jeffrey Vinik
- Winnipeg Jets – Owned by True North Sports & Entertainment: Mark Chipman, chairman
- Chicago Blackhawks – William Wirtz
- Edmonton Oilers – Owned by Rexall Sports: Daryl Katz, chairman
- Anaheim Ducks – Henry Samueli
- San Jose Sharks – Owned by San Jose Sports & Entertainment: Hasso Plattner, chairman

# THE JEWISH AGENDA

To use the word "agenda" is to again court charges of anti-Semitism. But a better word with which to describe the commonly-held ideology of Jewish-Americans is difficult to find. As stated in the introduction to this work, the vast majority of American Jews (and the vast majority of Jews occupying positions of power in this country) are liberal in nature and highly Zionist in their outlook on Israel. Also to reiterate from the introduction, this should not be misconstrued as stating that there is a Jewish conspiracy in effect in the United States. As has been repeated ad nauseam, Americans Jews simply display a common predilection for liberalism and are largely pro-Israel because they come from such a similar and exclusive background.

### *Jewish-American Liberalism*

The simplest way to demonstrate that Jewish-Americans are a nearly entirely liberal bunch is to analyze voting records. And the figures are nothing short of astonishing. Since 1960, no Republican candidate for president of the United States of America has received even forty percent of the Jewish vote (in 1980, Ronald Reagan received a modern-day high of thirty-nine percent).[68] In six of the fourteen presidential elections held since 1960 the Republican candidate has received less than twenty percent of the Jewish vote (in 1964, Barry Goldwater received a modern-day low of just ten percent).[69]

## Jewish Vote-Splits in Presidential Elections since 1960[70]

2012
Romney (R)      30%
Obama (D)       69%

2008
McCain (R)      22%
Obama (D)       78%

2004
Bush (R)        24%
Kerry (D)       76%

2000
Bush (R)        19%
Gore (D)        79%

1996
Dole (R)        16%
Clinton (D)     78%

1992
Bush (R)        11%
Clinton (D)     80%

1988
Bush (R)        35%
Dukakis (D)     64%

1984
Reagan (R)      31%
Mondale (D)     67%

1980
Reagan (R)     39%
Carter (D)     45%

1976
Ford (R)       27%
Carter (D)     71%

1972
Nixon (R)      35%
McGovern (D)   65%

1968
Nixon (R)      17%
Humphrey (D)   81%

1964
Goldwater (R)  10%
Johnson (D)    90%

1960
Nixon (R)      18%
Kennedy (D)    82%

Of course, the foregoing statistics merely illustrate that American Jews, as a whole, are overwhelmingly liberal from a political viewpoint. For our purposes, it more important to demonstrate that America's most powerful and influential Jews are also politically liberal.

### Jewish-American Liberalism in Action

We have already seen how a mindboggling number of positions of power and influence in the United States are occupied by Jews. It is important to now illustrate that same power and influence being utilized for liberal purposes.

## Law

The American Civil Liberties Union

- President: Susan Herman

The stated purpose of the ACLU is "to defend and preserve the individual rights and liberties guaranteed to every person in this country by the Constitution and laws of the United States." Of course, the Constitution is the source of much debate in terms of the specific rights it may or may not grant to American citizens. The ACLU has decided to interpret the Constitution as liberally as humanly possible – it favors affirmative action, is pro-choice on abortion, opposes the death penalty in all cases, supports flag-burning as a protected form of free-speech, and backs same-sex marriage.

Southern Poverty Law Center

- President: Richard Cohen

Originally, the SPLC was "an American nonprofit civil rights organization noted for its legal victories against white supremacist groups."[71] Now the group spends most of its energy on a cherished liberal cause: defending illegal aliens (also known as people who should not even be in the country). The SPLC has come out strongly against Arizona's anti-illegal immigration measures, the crux of which has been upheld by the United States Supreme Court.

Anti-Defamation League

- Director: Abraham Foxman

The ADL's "ultimate purpose is to secure justice and fair treatment to all citizens alike and to put an end forever to unjust and unfair discrimination against and ridicule of any sect or body of citizens."[72] The organization also now refers to itself as the nation's "premier civil rights/human relations agency," which seems like a stretch given that the ADL spends the vast majority of its time and resources on Jewish issues alone. To be fair, though, an increasing amount of its energy is being devoted to the liberal goal of instituting same-sex marriage in all fifty states.

Human Rights Watch

- Director: Kenneth Roth

"An international non-governmental organization that conducts research and advocacy on human rights," HRW is, to be more direct, a liberal body that fights for the world-wide abolition of capital punishment and expresses more sympathy for the rights of terrorists than for justice for the victims of terrorism.[73] These goals are not surprising given that arch-liberal George Soros has, in recent years, provided seventy-five percent of HRW's operating budget.

Education

In his seminal work, *God & Man at Yale*, the late William F. Buckley, Jr. was the first individual to point out the embarrassingly liberal state of American higher education. Buckley noted that many of his professors tried to inculcate in their charges anti-American, anti-capitalistic, and anti-religious values. While professing support for intellectual freedom, these same professors castigated any student or colleague that opposed their ultra-liberal principles. More than sixty years later, new books are still being published that clearly illustrate the same goings-on in the Ivy League in 2014.

As we have already seen, Jewish-Americans dominate the Ivy League, the zenith of our educational system. And they clearly bring their predominantly liberal values into the classroom. In fact, recent research indicates that Jewish professors are at the forefront of the effort to ensure that the Ivory Tower remains a bastion of liberalism. "Liberal Bias in Academia: The Role of Jewish Academics in the Creation and Maintenance of Academic Liberalism," a research paper written by Kevin MacDonald, covers this exact issue.[74] MacDonald has summarized the key findings of his research and they are as follows:

- Universities were relatively liberal even before the 1930s, but there was a pronounced shift to the left with the ascendancy of Jewish academics. This was particularly pronounced in the 1960s.
- The academic world is hierarchical, with top-down influence. Elite institutions are able to dominate the image of the ideal professor (political liberalism is a criterion of being ideal), and they are able to police the academic world to ensure that non-liberal attitudes are excluded, or at least marginalized.
- Jews are strongly overrepresented among academics, especially in the social sciences and especially at elite institutions. As a result, they have wielded disproportionate power in creating the image of ideal academic attitudes and behavior.
- The Jewish identification with the left originated in the early nineteenth century and has remained consistent in the Western diaspora. At least through the formative decade of the 1960s, political radicalism was entirely mainstream within the Jewish community and had a strong effect on the intellectual climate of elite college campuses at that time.
- Jews have indeed had legitimate complaints about their status in America (the long history of anti-Jewish attitudes and

a sense of exclusion in homogeneously white, Christian America), but they have been able to form cohesive, effective networks [in the academic world], typically by citing and promoting each other. Reflecting the importance of elite institutions for successful intellectual movements, Jews have had access to the most prestigious academic institutions.

- There has been a development in the academic world and beyond where Jews have made alliances with non-whites and with whites who also have complaints against the system (homosexuals, radical feminists)...In the academic world, the rise of the new Jewish elite was quickly followed by the establishment of departments and scholarly disciplines focused on minority and sexual grievance (i.e. black studies, gay studies). Collectively, these departments now wield a great deal of power within universities; they are reliable proponents of the leftist, multicultural world view.

- The ability of the left to discriminate in hiring and promotion means that there is a very great inertia in the system.

This last of MacDonald's points is reminiscent of Buckley's findings from over sixty years ago – the fact that supposedly open-minded liberal professors, both Jewish and Gentile, are ardent discriminators against the handful of conservative professors in place. In fact, a recent article published in the journal *Perspectives on Psychological Science* quantified this discrimination.[75] The article featured the results of a survey in which a third of the respondents, all self-professed liberal academicians, disclosed that they would intentionally work to prevent the hiring or advancement of an openly conservative colleague. The current state of affairs in the American educational system, as a whole, presents two problems: conservatives face discrimination and also that "any hint of political bias, whether conservative or liberal, necessarily flouts the standards of objectivity to which scholarship must adhere."[76]

When looking for concrete examples of Jewish professors inculcating liberal values in their students, we turn to a Jewish author, David Horowitz. In 2006, Horowitz published a controversial book, *The Professors: The 101 Most Dangerous Academics in America*, a listing of the most liberal professors in the country that was strewn with Jewish surnames.[77] Horowitz's hit-list included the following Jews:

- Bettina Aptheker – University of California – Charged by Horowitz with sympathizing with the fall of the Soviet Union, which actually seems logical as Aptheker was a full-fledged member of Communist Party USA in the 1960s.
- Joel Beinin – Stanford University - Charged by Horowitz with being an apologist for modern terrorism.
- Noam Chomsky – Massachusetts Institute of Technology – Charged by Horowitz with being "a pathological ayatollah of anti-American hate—and the leader of a treacherous fifth column left."
- Richard Falk – Princeton University – Charged by Horowitz with being "a prominent member of the International Association of Democratic Lawyers—a Communist front group."
- Eric Foner – Columbia University – Charged by Horowitz as being "an unabashed apologist for the Soviet system and an unforgiving historian of America." Horowitz continues, "Following the 9/11 attacks, Professor Foner focused not on the atrocity itself but on what he perceived to be the threat of an American response [against the attackers]."
- Todd Gitlin – Yale University – Charged by Horowitz with "Immersing students in the obscurantist texts of leftist icons like Jurgen Habermas so that they understand the oppressive nature of capitalist media." Horowitz goes on to state the Gitlin has spent decades "harboring the belief that his country is ultimately unworthy of his respect and even allegiance."

## The Media

"Gallup Polls show that most Americans do not have confidence in the mass media to report the news fully, accurately, and fairly. In 2011, a sixty percent majority reported a perception of media bias, with forty-seven percent saying mass media was too liberal and thirteen percent too conservative...According to Gallup, in every year since 2002 more Americans think the media shows liberal bias than think the media shows conservative bias."[78]

In the wake of the 2008 presidential election, much was made of the following statistics: "The Democratic Party received a total donation of $1,020,816 given by 1,160 employees of the three major broadcast television networks [ABC, CBS, and NBC], while the Republican Party received only $142,863 via 193 employees."[79]

But it was *The Media Elite*, a book published in 1986 by Linda Lichter, Robert Lichter, and Stanley Rothman, all of whom are Jewish, that remains the seminal analysis of liberal media bias.[80] The three writers "surveyed journalists at national media outlets such as the *New York Times*, the *Washington Post*, and the broadcast networks. The survey found that most of these journalists were Democratic voters, whose attitudes were well to the left of the general public on a variety of topics, including such hot-button social issues as abortion, affirmative action, and gay rights. Then they compared journalists' attitudes to their coverage of controversial issues such as the safety of nuclear power, school busing to promote racial integration, and the energy crisis of the 1970s. The authors concluded that the journalists' coverage of controversial issues reflected their own attitudes, and the predominance of political liberals in newsrooms therefore pushed news coverage in a liberal direction. They presented this tilt as a mostly unconscious process of like-minded individuals projecting their shared assumptions onto their interpretations of reality."[81]

It is, of course, no surprise that Jews are among the most liberal members of the media for the simple reason that the vast majority of Jews are liberal and the media is predominantly Jewish. In fact, Jews held five of ten spots, or fifty percent, in a recent ranking of the ten most liberally-biased members of the American media, which includes both newspaper and television journalism:[82]

- Howard Fineman – MSNBC – "As are all those that appear on the top ten list, Fineman is an apologist for "the one" [Barack Obama]…in fact, Fineman thinks Obama deserves to be placed on Mount Rushmore just for his 2010 state of the union speech… And do you want Democratic talking points? Well, Fineman plays the race card with the best of them….Fineman claims that everyone knows that the GOP is filled with racists and the party cannot win an argument on race."[83]

- Joe Klein – *Time* – "The examples of Klein's venomous pen are legion. Just to name a few: in 2007 he claimed that our effort in Iraq amounted to ethnic cleansing; in January of 2010 Klein called the American people 'too dumb to thrive' because they opposed Obama's wild spending spree; and in April he called Sarah Palin and Glenn Beck seditious just for having an opinion that stood opposite to the Klein-ian niche."[84]

- Paul Krugman – *New York Times* – "Krugman has seriously tried to claim that one of Barack Obama's biggest failings is that he *doesn't* blame Bush enough for his own failings. Unfortunately for Krugman…the facts show that blaming Bush has been a mainstay of nearly every policy speech and press conference Obama has made since he took office…In order to push the liberal perspective, Krugman isn't above a little dissembling in his work at the *New York Times*. Back in 2007, for instance, Krugman wrote a piece dismissing as nonsense the worry that Social Security was becoming insolvent…Krugman's ideas on economics have changed with each presidential administration – on one hand Krugman attacked Republican presidents for not reducing the deficit, yet during Clinton's and Obama's terms Krugman dismissed the importance of deficit reduction...Krugman is also well known to dismiss any ethics violations that are perpetrated by Democrats...When Charlie Rangel was finding that his multiple ethics violations were giving him trouble in the House of Representatives, Krugman waved his hand and pronounced the violations as having 'no national significance'...One wonders if Krugman would be so dismissive if similar ethics violations were perpetrated by a Republican."[85]

- Neil Steinberg – *Chicago Sun-Times* – "The king of left-wing lunacy in the Windy City has to be Neil Steinberg... Steinberg is a dogged abortion advocate...and has a real affinity for slamming conservatives. In short he believes in every left-wing trope in the book. And he seems to really dislike tea party folks, too... Steinberg charged that tea party attendees and anti-Obamacare activists were a kind of fifth column, an enemy within trying to undermine the operation of our government. He maintained that folks on the right...oppose Obama at every turn apparently out of pure racist spite. Steinberg obviously cannot grasp that there are real American principles behind opposition to Obama's wild expansion of big government."[86]

- Chuck Todd – NBC – "Over the last year, Todd has repeatedly gone out of his way to help Obama soften his failures and push the Democrat's talking points all while pretending at being a journalist. In an April 2009 'Today Show' segment with host Matt Lauer, Todd was keen to guide his viewers into dismissing as inconsequential the tea party events then being held by the hundreds all across the country. 'There's been some grassroots conservatives who have organized so-called tea parties around the country hoping the historical reference will help galvanize Americans against the president's economic ideas...But I tell you, the idea hasn't really caught on'...In 2010, Todd appeared on MSNBC's 'Daily Rundown' and waxed hopeful that Obama would use the British Petroleum oil spill to push new energy regulations on an already over-regulated nation. Echoing [then] White House Chief of Staff Rahm Emanuel's desire not to let a good crisis go to waste, Todd hoped that Obama could use the disaster to his own ends."[87]

## Entertainment

For proof of Hollywood's liberal agenda we again turn to a Jewish writer, Ben Shapiro, who "accuses Hollywood of rampant liberal bias in his book, *Primetime Propaganda*."[88] Shapiro writes, "The industry's elite uses broadcast to shape America in their own leftist image. I was shocked by the openness of the Hollywood crowd when it came to admitting anti-conservative discrimination inside the industry...They weren't ashamed of it. In fact, some were actually proud of it."[89]

Shapiro interviewed Marta Kauffman, co-creator of the television program 'Friends,' "who told Shapiro she hired a bunch of liberals to put out there what we believe. That included casting Newt Gingrich's lesbian sister to play a preacher at a lesbian wedding on the show."[90] Kauffman stated, "When we did the lesbian wedding, we knew there was going to be some flack...I have to say, when we cast Candice Gingrich as the minister of that wedding, there was a bit of a fuck you in it to the right-wing."[91]

Shapiro interviewed Vin DiBona, producer of the television program 'MacGyver,' who "agrees Hollywood has a liberal bias...I'm happy about it actually...the whole premise of [MacGyver] was anti-gun...MacGyver used his brain power and skill and science, and solved all the difficulties through ingenuity. No guns, no knives."[92]

Shapiro interviewed Gene Reynolds, co-creator of the television program 'MASH,' who says, "The program had a pacifist agenda. We wanted to point out the wastefulness of war."[93]

Shapiro interviewed Bill Bickley, a writer on the television program 'Happy Days,' who admits, "The show had a whole subtext against the Vietnam War...if you really look for it, you can find it."[94]

Finally, Shapiro concludes, "It was easy to get people to open up... There was a certain amount of stereotyping [in obtaining interviews from Hollywood insiders]. Many probably assumed that with a name like Shapiro and a Harvard Law credential...I would have to be a leftist. In Hollywood, talking to a Jew with a Harvard Law baseball cap is like talking to someone wearing an Obama pin... Hollywood [insiders] admit openly to messaging their product and to their scorn for conservative Americans."[95]

As with the media, it is no surprise that entertainment's leading liberals are Jewish because there are so many Jewish entertainers, and they include:

- Joy Behar – While on the television program 'The View,' Behar claimed that there are ways to get information out of terrorists other than interrogation methods such as waterboarding. "Pay them off," Behar said, "while suggesting offering a terrorist a $6 million book deal." This is the same individual who once stated, "It is really not easy to make fun of the Obamas because they're kind of really perfect, aren't they?"[96]
- Larry David – In one particular episode of his television program, 'Curb Your Enthusiasm,' "Jewish uber-liberal Larry David...pisses on the face of a painting of Jesus Christ, followed by mocking of Christians who believe the piss drop on the face of Jesus is a tear, thus they've witnessed a miracle."[97]

- Harrison Ford – "Ford was once asked what religion he and his brother had been raised in and he answered, 'Democrat, to be liberals of every stripe.'"[98]
- Maggie Gyllenhaal – The actress blamed the September 11, 2001, terrorist attacks on the United States itself, stating, "I think America has done reprehensible things and is responsible in some way."[99]
- Scarlett Johannson – "The young actress has shown her support for the Democratic Party by campaigning for presidential candidates John Kerry and Barack Obama."[100]
- Sean Penn – "The two-time Academy Award winner has traveled the world to denounce the country that made him rich and famous. He has been used as a propaganda tool by the Iranian regime, met with Cuban President Raul Castro, and went to Iraq as an anti-war activist. Penn was so close to Venezuelan strongman Hugo Chavez that the tyrant, in one of his televised speeches, read an open letter Penn wrote to George W. Bush condemning the Iraq War, calling for the president's impeachment and saying that Bush, Dick Cheney and Condoleezza Rice were villainously and criminally obscene people."[101]
- Gwyneth Paltrow – The actress "showed her support for Barack Obama and the Democratic party in a public service announcement for the 2008 elections."[102]
- Natalie Portman – The Israeli-born Portman is "An open supporter of the Democratic party. She campaigned for Democratic nominees John Kerry in 2004 and Hillary Clinton in 2008. She later campaigned for presidential nominee Barack Obama in the 2008 general election."[103]
- Steven Spielberg – "Spielberg is a well-known supporter of the Democratic Party. He's donated over $800,000 to the party and various nominees throughout the years."[104]
- Jerry Springer – "Day-time television personality Jerry Springer was once the Democratic mayor of Cincinnati

and has retained his status as a supporter of Democratic causes."[105]

- Barbara Streisand – "From her appearance on President Nixon's 'enemies list' to her singing performance at a fund-raising gala for Barack Obama, Barbra Streisand has a long history of political involvement. Most notable is her bank-rolling of left-wing causes, with the Streisand Foundation steering millions to groups promoting every liberal fantasy. Among her favorite causes are women's issues, nuclear dis-armament and the environment. She even donated $1 million to the William Jefferson Clinton Foundation to help solve global warming."[106]

## Culture

As detailed in my previous book, *On The Precipice: Constructing a Strategic Plan to Save the American Empire from Extinction*, liberals have, since the disastrous social revolution of the 1960s, waged an all-out war on traditional culture in the United States. And as of 2014, liberals now have a veritable monopoly of the influencing of our culture, especially through their control of the entertainment industry and the news media. Cherished liberal principles now include abortion, affirmative action, and same-sex marriage. The deleterious effect of the liberal agenda has even caused millions of Americans to believe that having children out of wedlock, divorce, and even drug use are all perfectly acceptable in modern America. All of this has combined to cause the complete breakdown of the traditional family unit, which remains the most devastating devel-opment in American society over the past fifty years. Furthermore, the generally-held liberal principle of blaming other people for one's own problems has caused several conflagrations in race rela-tions within the United States over the past several decades.

We have already seen how liberals, most of whom are Jewish, have a near monopoly on the various mediums (newspapers, movies, and television) through which culture can be influenced. It is now worth examining the manner in which ultra-liberal Jews formed the vanguard of the iconoclastic Hippie generation that proved so effective in destroying traditional social mores in America. Nearly all of the infamous figures of the 1960s counterculture are Jewish and they include the following:

- Lenny Bruce – "As a standup comedian…Bruce felt nothing was sacred. So he joked about racism, drugs, homophobia, nuclear testing, and abortion. What made him famous was his unmitigated use of profanity. He was arrested many times, for obscenity and narcotics."[107]
- Peter Coyote – "After a short apprenticeship at the San Francisco Actors' Workshop, [Coyote] joined the San Francisco Mime Troupe, a radical political street theater whose members were arrested for performing in parks without permits… From 1967 to 1975, Coyote became a prominent member of the San Francisco counterculture community and a founding member…of the Diggers, an anarchist group known for operating anonymously and without money."[108]
- Bernardine Dohrn – "Dohrn was a leader of the Weather Underground, a group that was responsible for the bombing of the United States Capitol, the Pentagon, and several police stations in New York City. As a member of the Weather Underground, Dohrn read a 'Declaration of a State of War' against the United States government, and was placed on the FBI's Most Wanted list, where she remained for three years. She now teaches at Northwestern Law School and is married to Bill Ayers, a co-founder of the Weather Underground, who was formerly a tenured professor at the University of Illinois at Chicago."[109]
- Allen Ginsberg – "Controversial Beat poet…who wrote about following your instincts and free love. Along with his friends Jack Kerouac and William S. Burroughs, he helped

define and document the activities of the Beat Generation. Ginsberg was active in the anti-war movement, appearing at rallies and also the 'Human Be-In.' Ginsberg is credited with coining the term 'Flower Power.'"[110]

- Abbie Hoffman – "Co-founder of the Yippies...One of the Chicago Seven. Outspoken advocate of anarchy, Hoffman challenged authority every chance he could. By his outrageous actions he tried to highlight the hypocrisies inherent in the system."[111]
- Paul Krassner – "Humorist, co-founding member of the Yippies, and publisher of *The Realist* newspaper, he's been called the founder of the underground press."[112]
- William Kunstler – "Self-described 'radical lawyer' and civil rights activist, known for his controversial clients. Kunstler was a board member of the American Civil Liberties Union and the co-founder of the Law Center for Constitutional Rights, the leading gathering place for radical lawyers in the country...Kunstler's defense of the Chicago Seven from 1969–1970 led the *New York Times* to label him 'the country's most controversial and, perhaps, best-known lawyer'... Kunstler is also well known for defending members of the...Black Panther Party, the Weather Underground, and the Attica Prison rioters."[113]
- Jerry Rubin – "Co-founder of the Yippies, one of the Chicago Seven. He and Abbie Hoffman pulled outrageous stunts to poke fun and make serious statements about our society. One such stunt was throwing dollar bills onto the floor of the New York Stock Exchange, disrupting trading as brokers got down on the floor to pick up the money."[114]

Fifty years after the heyday of these leaders of the catastrophic social revolution of the 1960s, ultra-liberal Jews still compromise the frontline ranks of those determined to obliterate any remaining semblance of traditional culture in the United States:

- Bill Maher – The host of the television program 'Real Time with Bill Maher,' "Maher is known for his political satire and socio-political commentary, which targets a wide swath of topics…He supports the legalization of prostitution, marijuana and same-sex marriage…He is also a critic of religion and is an advisory board member of Project Reason, an anti-religion organization."[115]
- Maury Povich – "Povich, with his self-titled television show, creates segments that glorify and sensationalize trashy American behavior. Examples include mothers who have sex with their daughter's boyfriends and shows about mothers who let their infants become really fat."[116]
- Jerry Springer – Springer, once described as a cultural sodomite, "helped pioneer the nasty television talk show genre. He and Maury Povich are rotting American culture."[117]
- Howard Stern – "Howard Stern's popular radio show makes fun of retarded people. His show also involves pornographic scenes that are usually performed on the Stern set and are then recounted live on public radio. He has also become a representative for First Amendment rights, but not because of any provocative political commentary. Rather, Stern is fighting for the right to make auditory pollution."[118]
- Jon Stewart – "Stewart is the host of 'The Daily Show,' a supposedly satirical news program that airs on television. 'The Daily Show,' however, is anything but satirical. Stewart passes daily judgment on conservative causes and does so without having to adhere to any realistic level of journalistic integrity because he broadcasts from a self-styled 'fake news desk.'" Stewart is a self-acknowledged admirer of the famous socialist Eugene Debs and also supports the legalization of marijuana and same-sex marriage.[119]
- Barbara Walters – "Walters claims to want to present a balanced view on American issues, yet puts a young and under-informed Elisabeth Hasselbeck against two pit bulls and sometimes three, depending on the co-host [of

her television program, 'The View']. Present the show as it is…a liberal talk show representing the liberal views of the Hollywood elite," the same liberal views destroying American culture.[120]

## Jewish-American Zionism

We have already seen how a mindboggling number of positions of power and influence in the United States are occupied by Jews. It is important to now illustrate that same power and influence being utilized for pro-Israeli purposes.

### Government

Controlling the federal government of the United States and exacting the most powerful lobby in the history of the world is the dual-manner in which Jewish-Americans successfully enact their Zionist beliefs, which is simply an unwavering support for Israel.

The easiest way to track Jewish influence in the federal government is to analyze the billions of dollars in foreign aid granted by the United States each year. America has come to influence diverse groups of people in all regions of the world by distributing record amounts of money. From 2001-2006, the most recent period for which reliable statistics are available, Israel was, in a landslide, the top recipient of foreign aid, having benefitted from an annual average of roughly $3 billion of American-taxpayer money.[121] During this same period, foreign aid to Israel easily outpaced that of Egypt (second place) by forty-six percent and Pakistan (third place) by an astounding six hundred percent.[122] The average annual foreign aid received by the Palestinians during that same period, while living in what President Jimmy Carter has described as "apartheid-like conditions" and supposedly being treated as equals in the Israeli-Palestinian conflict, was the relatively insulting amount of

$85 million.[123] Overall, the impact of America's one-sided distribution of foreign aid to Israel, already one of the world's wealthiest nations, has been to enrage the entire Muslim world, which comprises roughly a fifth of the planet's population, against the United States.[124] This has created an atmosphere conducive to the growth of international terrorism, whose sponsors can now strike in virtually any country on earth. In this manner, the distribution of American foreign aid can be seen as influencing all of the world's seven billion people.

While analyzing American foreign aid to Israel is quite an easy way to illustrate the influence of Zionist Jews in the federal government, it is not the most important. It is, rather, the Jewish stranglehold on positions of power within the president's inner-circle of advisors, and also inside the Department of Defense, that allows for the creation of an overall American foreign policy that has been unerringly beneficial to Israel, even when clearly detrimental to our own interests. Given the subject matter of this section, it is worth repeating the following analysis of Jewish influence in the executive branch of the federal government:

*Office of the President* – The Office of the President includes such positions as chief of staff, national security advisor, and senior advisor to the president. The men and women that fill these crucially important positions have direct access to the president on a routine basis and can therefore influence policy decisions in a profound way.

*–Chief of Staff -* In recent history, **no less than three of the past six chiefs of staff to the president, or fifty percent, have been Jewish** and include:

- Jacob Lew – Former chief of staff to Barack Obama
- Rahm Emanuel – Former chief of staff to Barack Obama
- Joshua Bolten – Former chief of staff to George W. Bush

*–National Security Advisor* – In recent history, **no less than two of the past six national security advisors, or thirty-three percent**, have been Jewish and include:

- Sandy Berger – Former national security advisor to Bill Clinton
- W. Anthony Lake – Former national security advisor to Bill Clinton

*–Senior Advisor to the President* – **Two of the past three senior advisors to the president, or sixty-seven percent, have been Jewish** and include:

- Valerie Jarrett – Current senior advisor to Barack Obama
- David Axelrod – Former senior advisor to Barack Obama

*Department of Defense* – "The mission of the Department of Defense is to deter war and to protect the security of our country." The Department of Defense is not only the largest government agency, but also the largest employer in the entire world with over three million people under its command. The budget of the Department of Defense has soared to over $550 billion annually, a figure which represents far more than half of the entire discretionary spending of the United States. **No less than four of the past thirteen secretaries of defense, or thirty-one percent, have been Jewish** and include:

- William Cohen – Former secretary of defense under Bill Clinton
- Caspar Weinberger – Former secretary of defense under Ronald Reagan
- Harold Brown – Former secretary of defense under Jimmy Carter
- James Schlesinger – Former secretary of defense under Richard Nixon

The absurd and pointless wars the United States has involved itself in since the terrorist attacks of September 11, 2001, including the Afghanistan War, the Iraq War, and the inevitable war with Iran that so many public figures are now calling for, all stem from the influence of Jewish figures inside the federal government clamoring for action designed to safeguard the interests and security of Israel. While considered anti-Semitic and untrue within the United States, the rest of the world, much less fearful of a Jewish backlash, considers this sentiment to be self-evident.

The following extended selection from an essay written by Professors John Mearsheimer and Stephen Walt, published in the *London Review of Books,* provides an excellent synopsis of the influence of powerful Jews in the federal government, as well as the manner in which the Jewish lobby ensures that America's foreign policy remains steadfastly pro-Israel:[125]

> "For the past several decades, and especially since the Six-Day War in 1967, the centerpiece of America's Middle East policy has been its relationship with Israel. The combination of unwavering support for Israel and the related effort to spread democracy throughout the region has inflamed Arab and Islamic opinion and jeopardized not only U.S. security, but that of much of the rest of the world.
>
> This situation has no equal in American political history. Why has the U.S. been willing to set aside its own security and that of many of its allies in order to advance the interests of another state? One might assume that the bond between the two countries was based on shared strategic interests or compelling moral imperatives, but neither explanation can account for the remarkable level of material and diplomatic support that the U.S. provides to Israel.

Instead, the thrust of U.S. policy in the region derives almost entirely from domestic politics, and especially the activities of the 'Israel Lobby'. Other special-interest groups have managed to skew foreign policy, but no lobby has managed to divert it as far from what the national interest would suggest, while simultaneously convincing Americans that U.S. interests and those of the other country – in this case, Israel – are essentially identical...

...Since the Yom Kippur War in 1973, Washington has provided Israel with a level of support dwarfing that given to any other state. It has been the largest annual recipient of direct economic and military assistance since 1976 and is the largest recipient in total since World War II, to the tune of well over $140 billion. Israel receives about $3 billion in direct assistance each year, roughly one-fifth of the foreign aid budget, and worth about $500 a year for every Israeli. This largesse is especially striking since Israel is now a wealthy industrial state with a per capita income roughly equal to that of South Korea or Spain.

Other recipients get their money in quarterly installments, but Israel receives its entire appropriation at the beginning of each fiscal year and can thus earn interest on it. Most recipients of aid given for military purposes are required to spend all of it in the U.S., but Israel is allowed to use roughly twenty-five per cent of its allocation to subsidize its own defense industry. It is the only recipient that does not have to account for how the aid is spent, which makes it virtually impossible to prevent the money from being used for purposes the U.S. opposes, such as building settlements in the West Bank.

Moreover, the U.S. has provided Israel with nearly $3 billion to develop weapons systems and given it access to such top-drawer weaponry as Blackhawk helicopters and F-16 jets. Finally, the U.S. gives Israel access to intelligence it denies to its NATO allies and turned a blind eye to Israel's acquisition of nuclear weapons [author's note: the technology for which it literally stole from the United States].

Washington also provides Israel with consistent diplomatic support. Since 1982, the U.S. has vetoed thirty-two [United Nations] Security Council resolutions critical of Israel, more than the total number of vetoes cast by all the other Security Council members. It blocks the efforts of Arab states to put Israel's nuclear arsenal on the International Atomic Energy Agency's agenda.

The U.S. comes to the rescue in wartime and takes Israel's side when negotiating peace. The Nixon administration protected it from the threat of Soviet intervention and re-supplied it during the Yom Kippur War. Washington was deeply involved in the negotiations that ended that war, as well as in the lengthy step-by-step process that followed, just as it played a key role in the negotiations that preceded and followed the 1993 Oslo Accords. In each case there was occasional friction between U.S. and Israeli officials, but the U.S. consistently supported the Israeli position. One American participant at Camp David in 2000 later said: 'Far too often, we functioned … as Israel's lawyer.' Finally, the Bush administration's ambition to transform the Middle East [was] at least partly aimed at improving Israel's strategic situation…

…This extraordinary generosity might be understandable if Israel were a vital strategic asset or if there were a compelling moral case for U.S. backing. But neither explanation is convincing. One might argue that Israel was an asset during the Cold War. By serving as America's proxy after 1967, it helped contain Soviet expansion in the region and inflicted humiliating defeats on Soviet clients like Egypt and Syria. It occasionally helped protect other U.S. allies (like King Hussein of Jordan) and its military prowess forced Moscow to spend more on backing its own client states. It also provided useful intelligence about Soviet capabilities.

Backing Israel was not cheap, however, and it complicated America's relations with the Arab world. For example, the decision to give $2.2 billion in emergency military aid during the Yom Kippur War triggered an OPEC oil embargo that inflicted considerable damage on Western economies. For all that, Israel's armed forces were not in a position to protect U.S. interests in the region. The U.S. could not, for example, rely on Israel when the Iranian Revolution in 1979 raised concerns about the security of oil supplies, and had to create its own Rapid Deployment Force instead.

The first Gulf War revealed the extent to which Israel was becoming a strategic burden. The U.S. could not use Israeli bases without rupturing the anti-Iraq coalition, and had to divert resources (e.g. Patriot missile batteries) to prevent Tel Aviv doing anything that might harm the alliance against Saddam Hussein. History repeated itself in 2003: although Israel was eager for the U.S. to attack Iraq, Bush could not ask it to help without triggering Arab opposition. So Israel stayed on the sidelines once again.

Beginning in the 1990s, and even more so after 9/11, U.S. support has been justified by the claim that both states are threatened by terrorist groups originating in the Arab and Muslim world, and by 'rogue states' that back these groups and seek weapons of mass destruction. This is taken to mean not only that Washington should give Israel a free hand in dealing with the Palestinians and not press it to make concessions until all Palestinian terrorists are imprisoned or dead, but that the U.S. should go after countries like Iran and Syria. Israel is thus seen as a crucial ally in the War on Terror, because its enemies are America's enemies. In fact, Israel is a liability in the War on Terror and the broader effort to deal with rogue states...

...More important, saying that Israel and the U.S. are united by a shared terrorist threat has the causal relationship backwards: the U.S. has a terrorism problem in good part because it is so closely allied with Israel, not the other way around. Support for Israel is not the only source of anti-American terrorism, but it is an important one, and it makes winning the War on Terror more difficult. There is no question that many al-Qaida leaders, including Osama bin Laden, are motivated by Israel's presence in Jerusalem and the plight of the Palestinians. Unconditional support for Israel makes it easier for extremists to rally popular support and to attract recruits...

...As for so-called rogue states in the Middle East, they are not a dire threat to vital U.S. interests, except inasmuch as they are a threat to Israel. Even if these states acquire nuclear weapons – which is obviously undesirable – neither America nor Israel could be blackmailed because the blackmailer could not carry out the threat without suffering overwhelming retaliation. The danger of a nuclear handover to terrorists is equally remote because a rogue state could not be sure the transfer would go undetected or that it would not be blamed and punished afterwards. The relationship with Israel actually makes it harder for the U.S. to deal with these states. Israel's nuclear arsenal is one reason some of its neighbors want nuclear weapons, and threatening them with regime change merely increases that desire...

...A final reason to question Israel's strategic value is that it does not behave like a loyal ally. Israeli officials frequently ignore U.S. requests and renege on promises (including pledges to stop building settlements and to refrain from 'targeted assassinations' of Palestinian leaders). Israel has provided sensitive military technology to potential rivals like China, in what the State Department's inspector-general called 'a systematic and growing pattern of unauthorized transfers'. According to the General Accounting Office, Israel also 'conducts the most aggressive espionage operations against the U.S. of any ally'. In addition to the case of Jonathan Pollard, who gave Israel large quantities of classified material in the early 1980s (which it reportedly passed on to the Soviet Union in return for more exit visas for Soviet Jews), a new controversy erupted in 2004 when it was revealed that a key Pentagon official named Larry Franklin had passed classified information to an Israeli diplomat. Israel is hardly the only country that spies on the U.S., but its willingness to spy on its principal patron casts further doubt on its strategic value...

...Israel's strategic value isn't the only issue. Its backers also argue that it deserves unqualified support because it is weak and surrounded by enemies; it is a democracy; the Jewish people have suffered from past crimes and therefore deserve special treatment; and Israel's conduct has been morally superior to that of its adversaries. On close inspection, none of these arguments is persuasive. There is a strong moral case for supporting Israel's existence, but that is not in jeopardy. Viewed objectively, its past and present conduct offers no moral basis for privileging it over the Palestinians.

Israel is often portrayed as David confronted by Goliath, but the converse is closer to the truth. Contrary to popular belief, the Zionists had larger, better equipped and better led forces during the 1947-49 War of Independence, and the Israel Defense Force won quick and easy victories against Egypt in 1956 and against Egypt, Jordan and Syria in 1967 – all of this before large-scale U.S. aid began flowing. Today, Israel is the strongest military power in the Middle East. Its conventional forces are far superior to those of its neighbors and it is the only state in the region with nuclear weapons. Egypt and Jordan have signed peace treaties with it, and Saudi Arabia has offered to do so. Syria has lost its Soviet patron, Iraq has been devastated by three disastrous wars and Iran is hundreds of miles away. The Palestinians barely have an effective police force, let alone an army that could pose a threat to Israel. According to a 2005 assessment by Tel Aviv University's Jaffee Center for Strategic Studies, 'the strategic balance decidedly favors Israel, which has continued to widen the qualitative gap between its own military capability and deterrence powers and those of its neighbors.' If backing the underdog were a compelling motive, the United States would be supporting Israel's opponents.

That Israel is a fellow democracy surrounded by hostile dictatorships cannot account for the current level of aid: there are many democracies around the world, but none receives the same lavish support. The U.S. has overthrown democratic governments in the past and supported dictators when this was thought to advance its interests – it has good relations with a number of dictatorships today.

Some aspects of Israeli democracy are at odds with core American values. Unlike the U.S., where people are supposed to enjoy equal rights irrespective of race, religion or ethnicity, Israel was explicitly founded as a Jewish state and citizenship is based on the principle of blood kinship. Given this, it is not surprising that its 1.3 million Arabs are treated as second-class citizens, or that a recent Israeli government commission found that Israel behaves in a 'neglectful and discriminatory' manner towards them. Its democratic status is also undermined by its refusal to grant the Palestinians a viable state of their own or full political rights...

...A third justification is the history of Jewish suffering in the Christian West, especially during the Holocaust. Because Jews were persecuted for centuries and could feel safe only in a Jewish homeland, many people now believe that Israel deserves special treatment from the United States. The country's creation was undoubtedly an appropriate response to the long record of crimes against Jews, but it also brought about fresh crimes against a largely innocent third party: the Palestinians. This was well understood by Israel's early leaders. David Ben-Gurion told Nahum Goldmann, the president of the World Jewish Congress, 'If I were an Arab leader I would never make terms with Israel. That is natural: we have taken their country ... We come from Israel, but two thousand years ago, and what is that to them? There has been anti-Semitism, the Nazis, Hitler, Auschwitz, but was that their fault? They only see one thing: we have come here and stolen their country. Why should they accept that?'

Since then, Israeli leaders have repeatedly sought to deny the Palestinians' national ambitions. When she was prime minister, Golda Meir famously remarked that 'there is no such thing as a Palestinian.' Pressure from extremist violence and Palestinian population growth has forced subsequent Israeli leaders to disengage from the Gaza Strip and consider other territorial compromises, but not even Yitzhak Rabin was willing to offer the Palestinians a viable state. Ehud Barak's purportedly generous offer at Camp David [in 2000] would have given them only a disarmed set of Bantustans under de facto Israeli control. The tragic history of the Jewish people does not obligate the U.S. to help Israel today no matter what it does...

...Israel's backers also portray it as a country that has sought peace at every turn and shown great restraint even when provoked. The Arabs, by contrast, are said to have acted with great wickedness. Yet on the ground, Israel's record is not distinguishable from that of its opponents. Ben-Gurion acknowledged that the early Zionists were far from benevolent towards the Palestinian Arabs, who resisted their encroachments – which is hardly surprising, given that the Zionists were trying to create their own state on Arab land. In the same way, the creation of Israel in 1947-48 involved acts of ethnic cleansing, including executions, massacres and rapes by Jews, and Israel's subsequent conduct has often been brutal, belying any claim to moral superiority. Between 1949 and 1956, for example, Israeli security forces killed between 2700 and 5000 Arab infiltrators, the overwhelming majority of them unarmed. The IDF murdered hundreds of Egyptian prisoners of war in both the 1956 and 1967 wars, while in 1967, it expelled between 100,000 and 260,000 Palestinians from the newly conquered West Bank, and drove 80,000 Syrians from the Golan Heights.

The Palestinian resort to terrorism is wrong, but it isn't surprising. The Palestinians believe they have no other way to force Israeli concessions. As Ehud Barak once admitted, had he been born a Palestinian, he 'would have joined a terrorist organization...'

...So if neither strategic nor moral arguments can account for America's support for Israel, how are we to explain it? The explanation is the unmatched power of the Israel Lobby. We use 'the Lobby' as shorthand for the loose co-alition of individuals and organizations who actively work to steer U.S. foreign policy in a pro-Israel direction. This is not meant to suggest that 'the Lobby' is a unified movement with a central leadership, or that individuals within it do not disagree on certain issues. Not all Jewish-Americans are part of the Lobby because Israel is not a salient issue for many of them...

Not surprisingly, Jewish-American leaders often consult Israeli officials to make sure that their actions advance Israeli goals. As one activist from a major Jewish organization wrote, 'It is routine for us to say, this is our policy on a certain issue, but we must check what the Israelis think. We as a community do it all the time.' There is a strong prejudice against criticizing Israeli policy and putting pressure on Israel is considered out of order. Edgar Bronfman, Sr., the president of the World Jewish Congress, was accused of 'perfidy' when he wrote a letter to President Bush in mid-2003 urging him to persuade Israel to curb construction of its controversial security fence. His critics said that 'it would be obscene at any time for the president of the World Jewish Congress to lobby the president of the United States to re-sist policies being promoted by the government of Israel.'

Similarly, when the president of the Israel Policy Forum, Seymour Reich, advised Condoleezza Rice in November 2005 to ask Israel to reopen a critical border crossing in the Gaza Strip, his action was denounced as 'irresponsible': 'There is,' his critics said, 'absolutely no room in the Jewish mainstream for actively canvassing against the security-re-lated policies of Israel...'

...The Lobby pursues two broad strategies. First, it wields its significant influence in Washington, pressuring both Congress and the executive branch. Whatever an individual lawmaker or policymaker's own views may be, the Lobby tries to make supporting Israel the 'smart' choice. Second, it strives to ensure that public discourse portrays Israel in a positive light, by repeating myths about its founding and by promoting its point of view in policy debates. The goal is to prevent critical comments from getting a fair hearing in the political arena. Controlling the debate is essential to guaranteeing U.S. support because a candid discussion of U.S.-Israeli relations might lead Americans to favor a different policy.

A key pillar of the Lobby's effectiveness is its influence in Congress, where Israel is virtually immune from criticism. This in itself is remarkable because Congress rarely shies away from contentious issues. Where Israel is concerned, however, potential critics fall silent. One reason is that some key members are Christian Zionists like Dick Armey, who said in September 2002, 'My number one priority in foreign policy is to protect Israel.' One might think that the number one priority for any congressman would be to protect America. There are also Jewish senators and congressmen who work to ensure that U.S. foreign policy supports Israel's interests.

Another source of the Lobby's power is its use of pro-Israel congressional staffers. As Morris Amitay, a former head of AIPAC [American Israel Public Affairs Committee], once admitted, 'there are a lot of guys at the working level up here – on Capitol Hill – who happen to be Jewish, who are willing ... to look at certain issues in terms of their Jewishness ... These are all guys who are in a position to make the decision in these areas for those senators ... You can get an awful lot done just at the staff level.'

AIPAC itself, however, forms the core of the Lobby's influence in Congress. Its success is due to its ability to reward legislators and congressional candidates who support its agenda and to punish those who challenge it. Money is critical to U.S. elections and AIPAC makes sure that its friends get strong financial support from the many pro-Israel political action committees. Anyone who is seen as hostile to Israel can be sure that AIPAC will direct campaign contributions to his or her political opponents. AIPAC also organizes letter-writing campaigns and encourages newspaper editors to endorse pro-Israel candidates...

...AIPAC's influence on Capitol Hill goes even further. According to Douglas Bloomfield, a former AIPAC staff member, 'it is common for members of Congress and their staffs to turn to AIPAC first when they need information, before calling the Library of Congress, the Congressional Research Service, committee staff or administration experts.' More important, he notes that AIPAC is 'often called on to draft speeches, work on legislation, advise on tactics, perform research, collect co-sponsors and marshal votes.'

The bottom line is that AIPAC, a de facto agent for a foreign government, has a stranglehold on Congress, with the result that U.S. policy towards Israel is not debated there, even though that policy has important consequences for the entire world. In other words, one of the three main branches of the government is firmly committed to supporting Israel. As one former Democratic senator, Ernest Hollings, noted on leaving office, 'you cannot have an Israeli policy other than what AIPAC gives you around here.' Or as Ariel Sharon once told an American audience, 'when people ask me how they can help Israel, I tell them, help AIPAC.'

Thanks in part to the influence Jewish voters have on presidential elections, the Lobby also has significant leverage over the executive branch. Although they make up fewer than three percent of the population, they make large campaign donations to candidates from both parties. The *Washington Post* once estimated that Democratic presidential candidates 'depend on Jewish supporters to supply as much as sixty percent of the money.' And because Jewish voters have high turn-out rates and are concentrated in key states like California, Florida, Illinois, New York and Pennsylvania, presidential candidates go to great lengths not to antagonize them.

Key organizations in the Lobby make it their business to ensure that critics of Israel do not get important foreign policy jobs. Jimmy Carter wanted to make George Ball his first secretary of state, but knew that Ball was seen as critical of Israel and that the Lobby would oppose the appointment. In this way any aspiring policymaker is encouraged to become an overt supporter of Israel, which is why public critics of Israeli policy have become an endangered species in the foreign policy establishment...

During the Clinton administration, Middle East policy was largely shaped by officials with close ties to Israel or to prominent pro-Israel organizations; among them, Martin Indyk, the former deputy director of research at AIPAC and co-founder of the pro-Israel Washington Institute for Near East Policy (WINEP); Dennis Ross, who joined WINEP after leaving government in 2001; and Aaron Miller, who has lived in Israel and often visits the country. These men were among Clinton's closest advisers at the Camp David summit in July 2000. Although all three supported the Oslo peace process and favored the creation of a Palestinian state, they did so only within the limits of what would be acceptable to Israel. The American delegation took its cues from Ehud Barak, coordinated its negotiating positions with Israel in advance, and did not offer independent proposals. Not surprisingly, Palestinian negotiators complained that they were 'negotiating with two Israeli teams – one displaying an Israeli flag, and one an American flag.'

The situation [was] even more pronounced in the Bush administration, whose ranks have included such fervent advocates of the Israeli cause as Elliot Abrams, John Bolton, Douglas Feith, I. Lewis ('Scooter') Libby, Richard Perle, Paul Wolfowitz and David Wurmser [author's note: all of whom are Jewish except for Bolton]...these officials have consistently pushed for policies favored by Israel and backed by organizations in the Lobby.

The Lobby does not want an open debate, of course, because that might lead Americans to question the level of support they provide. Accordingly, pro-Israel organizations work hard to influence the institutions that do most to shape popular opinion.

The Lobby's perspective prevails in the mainstream media: 'the debate among Middle East pundits,' the journalist Eric Alterman writes, 'is dominated by people who cannot imagine criticizing Israel'. He lists sixty-one columnists and commentators who can be counted on to support Israel reflexively and without qualification. Conversely, he found just five pundits who consistently criticize Israeli actions or endorse Arab positions. Newspapers occasionally publish guest op-eds challenging Israeli policy, but the balance of opinion clearly favors the other side.

Editorial bias is also found in papers like the *New York Times*, which occasionally criticizes Israeli policies and sometimes concedes that the Palestinians have legitimate grievances, but is not even-handed. In his memoirs, the paper's former executive editor, Max Frankel [author's note: who is Jewish], acknowledges the impact his own attitude had on his editorial decisions: 'I was much more deeply devoted to Israel than I dared to assert ... Fortified by my knowledge of Israel and my friendships there, I myself wrote most of our Middle East commentaries. As more Arab than Jewish readers recognized, I wrote them from a pro-Israel perspective...'

...The Israeli side also dominates the think tanks which play an important role in shaping public debate, as well as actual policy. The Lobby created its own think tank in 1985, when Martin Indyk helped to found WINEP. Although WINEP plays down its links to Israel, claiming instead to provide a 'balanced and realistic' perspective on Middle East issues, it is funded and run by individuals deeply committed to advancing Israel's agenda.

The Lobby's influence extends well beyond WINEP, however. Over the past twenty-five years, pro-Israel forces have established a commanding presence at the American Enterprise Institute, the Brookings Institution, the Center for Security Policy, the Foreign Policy Research Institute, the Heritage Foundation, the Hudson Institute, the Institute for Foreign Policy Analysis and the Jewish Institute for National Security Affairs (JINSA). These think tanks employ few, if any, critics of U.S. support for Israel...

...No discussion of the Lobby would be complete without an examination of one of its most powerful weapons: the charge of anti-Semitism. Anyone who criticizes Israel's

actions or argues that pro-Israel groups have significant influence over U.S. Middle East policy – an influence AIPAC
celebrates – stands a good chance of being labeled an anti-Semite. Indeed, anyone who merely claims that there *is*
an Israel Lobby runs the risk of being charged with anti-
Semitism, even though the Israeli media refer to America's
'Jewish Lobby'. In other words, the Lobby first boasts of its
influence and then attacks anyone who calls attention to
it. It's a very effective tactic; anti-Semitism is something no
one wants to be accused of.

Europeans have been more willing than Americans to
criticize Israeli policy, which some people attribute to a re-
surgence of anti-Semitism in Europe. 'We are getting to a
point,' the U.S. ambassador to the European Union said
in early 2004, 'where it is as bad as it was in the 1930s.'
Measuring anti-Semitism is a complicated matter, but the
weight of evidence points in the opposite direction. In the
spring of 2004, when accusations of European anti-Semitism
filled the air in America, separate surveys of European public opinion conducted by the U.S.-based Anti-Defamation
League and the Pew Research Center for the People and
the Press found that it was in fact declining. In the 1930s,
by contrast, anti-Semitism was not only widespread among
Europeans of all classes, but considered quite acceptable.
Israel's advocates, when pressed to go beyond mere asser-
tion, claim that there is a 'new anti-Semitism', which they
equate with criticism of Israel. In other words, criticize
Israeli policy and you are by definition an anti-Semite…

…U.S. officials have offered mild criticism of a few Israeli actions, but have done little to help create a viable Palestinian
state. Sharon has Bush 'wrapped around his little finger',
the former national security adviser Brent Scowcroft said in
October 2004. If Bush tries to distance the U.S. from Israel,

or even criticizes Israeli actions in the occupied territories, he is certain to face the wrath of the Lobby and its supporters in Congress. Democratic presidential candidates understand that these are facts of life, which is the reason John Kerry went to great lengths to display unalloyed support for Israel in 2004, and why Hillary Clinton does the same thing today...

...Maintaining U.S. support for Israel's policies against the Palestinians is essential as far as the Lobby is concerned, but its ambitions do not stop there. It also wants America to help Israel remain the dominant regional power. The Israeli government and pro-Israel groups in the United States have worked together to shape the administration's policy towards Iraq, Syria and Iran, as well as its grand scheme for re-ordering the Middle East.

Pressure from Israel and the Lobby was not the only factor behind the decision to attack Iraq in March 2003, but it was critical. Some Americans believe that this was a war for oil, but there is hardly any direct evidence to support this claim. Instead, the war was motivated in good part by a desire to make Israel more secure. According to Philip Zelikow, a former member of the president's Foreign Intelligence Advisory Board, the executive director of the 9/11 Commission, and a [former] counselor to Condoleezza Rice, 'the real threat from Iraq was not a threat to the United States...The unstated threat was the threat against Israel...'

...At a key meeting with Bush at Camp David on September 15, 2001, Paul Wolfowitz advocated attacking Iraq before Afghanistan, even though there was no evidence that Saddam was involved in the [9/11] attacks on the U.S. and bin Laden was known to be in Afghanistan. Bush rejected his advice and chose to go after Afghanistan instead, but war with Iraq was now regarded as a serious possibility and on November 21, 2001, the president charged military planners with developing concrete plans for an invasion...

...Pro-Israel forces have long been interested in getting the U.S. military more directly involved in the Middle East. But they had limited success during the Cold War because America acted as an 'off-shore balancer' in the region. Most forces designated for the Middle East, like the Rapid Deployment Force, were kept 'over the horizon' and out of harm's way. The idea was to play local powers off against each other – which is why the Reagan administration supported Saddam against revolutionary Iran during the Iran-Iraq War – in order to maintain a balance favorable to the U.S...

...Israelis tend to describe every threat in the starkest terms, but Iran is widely seen as their most dangerous enemy because it is the most likely to acquire nuclear weapons. Virtually all Israelis regard an Islamic country in the Middle East with nuclear weapons as a threat to their existence.

Ariel Sharon began pushing the U.S. to confront Iran in November 2002 in an interview in the *New York Times*. Describing Iran as the 'center of world terror' and bent on acquiring nuclear weapons, he declared that the Bush administration should put the strong-arm on Iran 'the day after' it conquered Iraq. In late April 2003, *Ha'aretz* reported that the Israeli ambassador in Washington was calling for regime change in Iran. The overthrow of Saddam, he noted, was 'not enough'. In his words, America 'has to follow through. We still have great threats of that magnitude coming from Syria, coming from Iran...'

...The [United States] has responded to the Lobby's pressure by working overtime to shut down Iran's nuclear program. But Washington has had little success and Iran seems determined to create a nuclear arsenal. As a result, the Lobby has intensified its pressure. Op-eds and other articles now warn of imminent dangers from a nuclear Iran, caution against any appeasement of a 'terrorist' regime, and hint darkly of preventive action should diplomacy fail...Israeli officials also warn they may take preemptive action should Iran continue down the nuclear road, threats partly intended to keep Washington's attention on the issue.

One might argue that Israel and the Lobby have not had much influence on policy towards Iran because the U.S. has its own reasons for keeping Iran from going nuclear. There is some truth in this, but Iran's nuclear ambitions do not pose a direct threat to the United States. If Washington could live with a nuclear Soviet Union, a nuclear China, or even a nuclear North Korea, it can live with a nuclear Iran. And that is why the Lobby must keep up constant pressure on politicians to confront Tehran. Iran and the U.S. would hardly be allies if the Lobby did not exist, but U.S. policy would be more temperate and preventive war would not be a serious option...

...It is not surprising that Israel and its American supporters want the U.S. to deal with any and all threats to Israel's security. If their efforts to shape U.S. policy succeed, Israel's enemies will be weakened or overthrown, Israel will get a free hand with the Palestinians, and the U.S. will do most of the fighting, dying, rebuilding and paying. But even if the U.S. fails to transform the Middle East and finds itself in conflict with an increasingly radicalized Arab and Islamic world, Israel will end up protected by the world's only superpower. This is not a perfect outcome from the Lobby's point of view, but it is obviously preferable to Washington distancing itself or using its leverage to force Israel to make peace with the Palestinians.

Can the Lobby's power be curtailed? One would like to think so given the Iraq debacle, the obvious need to rebuild America's image in the Arab and Islamic world, and the recent revelations about AIPAC officials passing U.S. government secrets to Israel. One might also think that Yasir Arafat's death and the election of the more moderate Mahmoud Abbas would cause Washington to press vigorously and even-handedly for a peace agreement. In short, there are ample grounds for leaders to distance themselves from the Lobby and adopt a Middle East policy more consistent with broader U.S. interests. In particular, using American power to achieve a just peace between Israel and the Palestinians would help advance the cause of democracy in the region.

But that is not going to happen – not soon anyway. AIPAC and its allies (including Christian Zionists) have no serious opponents in the lobbying world. They know it has become more difficult to make Israel's case today and they are responding by taking on staff and expanding their activities. Besides, American politicians remain acutely sensitive to campaign contributions and other forms of political pressure, and major media outlets are likely to remain sympathetic to Israel no matter what it does.

The Lobby's influence causes trouble on several fronts. It increases the terrorist danger that all states face – including America's European allies. It has made it impossible to end the Israeli-Palestinian conflict, a situation that gives extremists a powerful recruiting tool, increases the pool of potential terrorists and sympathizers, and contributes to Islamic radicalism in Europe and Asia.

Equally worrying, the Lobby's campaign for regime change in Iran and Syria could lead the U.S. to attack those countries with potentially disastrous effects...At a minimum, the Lobby's hostility towards Syria and Iran makes it almost impossible for Washington to enlist them in the struggle against al-Qaeda and the Iraqi insurgency, where their help is badly needed.

There is a moral dimension here as well. Thanks to the Lobby, the United States has become the de facto enabler of Israeli expansion in the occupied territories, making it complicit in the crimes perpetrated against the Palestinians. This situation undercuts Washington's efforts to promote democracy abroad and makes it look hypocritical when it presses other states to respect human rights. U.S. efforts to limit nuclear proliferation appear equally hypocritical given its willingness to accept Israel's nuclear arsenal, which only encourages Iran and others to seek a similar capability.

The Lobby's campaign to quash debate about Israel is unhealthy for democracy. Silencing skeptics by organizing blacklists and boycotts – or by suggesting that critics are anti-Semites – violates the principle of open debate on which democracy depends. The inability of Congress to conduct a genuine debate on these important issues paralyzes the entire process of democratic deliberation. Israel's backers should be free to make their case and to challenge those who disagree with them, but efforts to stifle debate by intimidation must be roundly condemned.

Finally, the Lobby's influence has been bad for Israel. Its ability to persuade Washington to support an expansionist agenda has discouraged Israel from seizing opportunities – including a peace treaty with Syria and a prompt and full implementation of the Oslo Accords – that would have saved Israeli lives and shrunk the ranks of Palestinian extremists. Denying the Palestinians their legitimate political rights certainly has not made Israel more secure, and the long campaign to kill or marginalize a generation of Palestinian leaders has empowered extremist groups like Hamas and reduced the number of Palestinian leaders who would be willing to accept a fair settlement...Israel itself would probably be better off if the Lobby were less powerful and U.S. policy more even-handed."[126]

Within the United States, the Jews working most vigorously in the interests of Israel include the following:

- Elliot Abrams – Former deputy national security advisor under George W. Bush and former assistant secretary of state under Ronald Reagan, Abrams is now leading the call for preemptive strikes on Iran's nuclear facilities.
- Alan Dershowitz – Harvard professor has made defending Israel his life's work, published *The Case for Israel* in 2003, and smears as anti-Semitic anyone who questions Jewish influence in America.
- Michael Kassen – President of AIPAC, the most powerful lobbying group in the United States, which suppresses any and all anti-Israel chatter.
- Richard Perle – Former chairman of the Defense Policy Board under George W. Bush and former assistant secretary of defense under Ronald Reagan, Perle was an early advocate of regime change in Iraq and has proposed armed invasions of Iran and Lebanon.

- Paul Wolfowitz – Former deputy secretary of defense under George W. Bush, Wolfowitz was the leading voice in the administration for invading Iraq in 2003.

# DEALING WITH OPPOSITION TO JEWISH INFLUENCE

There are five stratagems utilized by American Jewry to deal with opposition to Jewish power in the United States and support for Israel in the international arena:

1. Monopolizing Positions of Power and Influence in American Society
2. Exerting a Powerful Lobbying Presence
3. Smearing Opponents as anti-Semitic
4. Exploiting the Holocaust
5. Exploiting the Bible

### Monopolizing Positions of Power and Influence in American Society

The primary purpose of this work has been to quantify Jewish power and influence in American society, which far outdistances the percentage of the overall population that Jews comprise. Merely controlling the positions of power that they do allows America's Jews to prevent nearly all thought opposing Jewish interests from seeing the light of day. And, quite obviously, Jews can use the mediums they control (newspapers, movies, and television) to disseminate their own favorable propaganda.

To once again prove that Jews do indeed exert massive control over the most important segments of American society, it is worth reiterating several crucial findings from the quantitative analysis conducted earlier. When reviewing the following statistics, keep in mind that Jews form roughly two percent of the entire population of the United States.

Government

- **No less than three of the past six chiefs of staff to the president of the United States, or fifty percent, have been Jewish**
- **No less than two of the past six national security advisors, or thirty-three percent, have been Jewish**
- **Two of the past three senior advisors to the president of the United States, or sixty-seven percent, have been Jewish**
- **The Office of Management and Budget is headed by a director, of which no less than five of the past eleven, or forty-five percent, have been Jewish**
- **The Council of Economic Advisors is headed by a chairman, of which no less than eleven of the past twenty, or fifty-five percent, have been Jewish**
- **The National Economic Council is headed by a director, of which no less than five of the past nine, or fifty-six percent, have been Jewish**
- **The World Bank has had just twelve presidents since its founding in 1946, of which no less than five, or forty-two percent, have been Jewish (as stated earlier, the World Bank is a non-governmental institution, yet maintains close ties to several agencies of the federal government).**
- **The vice president has his own chief of staff, of which no less than four of the past eight, or fifty percent, have been Jewish**
- **No less than four of the past thirteen secretaries of defense, or thirty-one percent, have been Jewish**

- **No less than two of the past twelve attorneys general, or seventeen percent, have been Jewish**
- **No less than five of the past seven secretaries of the treasury, or seven-one percent, have been Jewish**
- **No less than four of the past six chairs of the Federal Reserve, or sixty-seven percent, have been Jewish**
- **The SEC is headed by a chairperson, of which no less than two of the past three, or sixty-seven percent, have been Jewish**
- **Three of the nine current Supreme Court justices, or thirty-three percent, are Jewish**
- **Michael Bloomberg and Rahm Emmanuel are the Jewish mayors of two of the three largest cities in America, New York City (8.3 million people) and Chicago (2.7 million people).**
- **Three of New York City's past five mayors, or sixty percent, have been Jewish**

Law

**The most powerful and influential law groups in the United States include the following, all of which have Jewish presidents and/or directors:**

- Anti-Defamation League
- American Center for Law and Justice
- American Civil Liberties Union
- Human Rights Watch
- Leadership Conference on Civil and Human Rights
- Southern Poverty Law Center

Academia

- **No less than five of the eight Ivy League institutions, or sixty-three percent, currently have Jewish presidents**

- No less than twenty-five of America's fifty most influential think tanks, or fifty percent, have Jewish presidents and/or directors
- A recent ranking of the world's one hundred greatest living intellectuals included thirty-six Americans, of whom twenty-two, or sixty-one percent, are Jewish

## Media

- No less than fourteen of America's top twenty-five newspapers, or fifty-six percent, are owned, published, or edited by Jews
- A recent report listed a total of sixty-nine newspaper columns being syndicated throughout the United States, of which twenty-seven, or thirty-nine percent, are written by Jewish journalists.
- All four of the major television broadcasting networks in the United States, or one hundred percent, are headed by American Jews.
- All three of the highest-rated cable news channels in America, or one hundred percent, have Jewish chairmen or CEOs.

## Business

- Analysis of the 2012 *Fortune* 100 list shows that no less than nineteen of these one hundred elite corporations, or nineteen percent, have Jewish chairmen or CEOs.
- Analysis of a recent ranking of the top thirty hedge funds in the United States shows that twenty-two of thirty, or seventy-three percent, are managed by Jews.
- Analysis of a recent ranking of the top thirty private equity groups in the United States shows that nine of thirty, or thirty percent, are managed by Jews.

- **Analysis of the 2012 *Forbes* 400 list shows that no less than one hundred thirty of the four hundred richest Americans, or thirty-three percent, are Jewish.**

## Entertainment

- **The "Big Six" control the movie industry and, in terms of movie production, each corporation has a parent division and a major studio subsidiary. Nine out of twelve of these divisions and subsidiaries, or seventy-five percent, are run by Jewish-Americans.**
- **Over the past several years, a frenetic pace of mergers and acquisitions has resulted in the consolidation of the music industry into just three major recording companies, known as the "Big Three." All of the "Big Three" recording companies, or one hundred percent, are headed by American Jews.**

*Exerting a Powerful Lobbying Presence*

Thanks to the extended passage provided to us by John Mearsheimer and Stephen Walt, we have already seen how the Jewish lobby effects the policy decisions it so desires in the United States, which is basically to blackmail elected officials through the withholding of campaign contributions and the supporting of opposition candidates against those individuals that do not toe the line, as well as charging with anti-Semitism any politician with the courage to speak out against Jewish dominance. But a closer look at the American Israel Public Affairs Committee (AIPAC) is still necessary.

"Washington is a city of acronyms, and today one of the best-known in Congress is AIPAC," former Representative Paul Findley stated in his book, *They Dare to Speak Out: People and Institutions Confront*

*Israel's Lobby.*[127] Findley continues, "The mere mention of it brings a sober, if not furtive look, to the face of anyone on Capitol Hill. AIPAC...is now the preeminent power in Washington lobbying."[128]

> "Its job is to maintain America's support and favorable opinion towards Israel. It has an annual budget of $60 million, a staff of 275, and is backed up by over 100,000 grassroots members. It also has an endowment of $135 million and a new $80 million headquarters on Capitol Hill. Almost every major U.S. politician, including Barack Obama, has spoken at [AIPAC's] conference...
>
> ...This begs a simple question – why is the mighty United States so scared of little old Israel? They reason is the determined influence of the Jewish lobby. Indeed, the influence is so strong that to publicly criticize Israel is a social and political taboo. Journalists and academics have quickly learned that being pro-Israel in the U.S. makes it a lot easier to further your career.
>
> But it's the politicians who have the most to fear. It is now commonly-held knowledge in the halls of Washington that if a politician ever spoke out for the rights of the Palestinians on the Congress or Senate floor, that would be the end of their career. They would be shunned by other politicians, making any legislation they propose, particularly for their state, almost impossible to get passed. But more significantly, their opponent in the next election would be flooded with political donations, and an advertising campaign would likely label them a supporter of terrorism and an enemy of Israel. The advertising and anti-Semitic accusations from the opponent, not to mention the lack of progress in Washington, would collectively make the election unwinnable. The threat is a reality for politicians thanks to AIPAC's highly organized band of followers."[129]

"Q: If it's true that AIPAC dictates American policy, is that a criticism of AIPAC, or is it a criticism of the people who actually carry out that foreign policy? Shouldn't they be open to more criticism than AIPAC?

A: I'm not criticizing any member of Congress because I see the pressures on them. But if anyone wants to be elected or re-elected to Congress it would be inconceivable that they would say, 'If I'm elected I'm going to take a balanced position between Israel and the Palestinians,' or that they would say 'I'm going to hope that Israel would withdraw from occupied territories and comply with international law,' or to say 'I'm going to make sure that the Palestinian human rights are protected.' It would be political suicide, which is unfortunate in my opinion. But I'm not criticizing either AIPAC or the candidates. It's just the way of life in this nation."[130]

–Jimmy Carter

The Jewish lobby dictates both America's domestic and foreign affairs. Thankfully, and as we have already done throughout this work, we can turn to American Jews, Israelis, and international leaders for commentary on this indisputable fact. The following is a list of particularly piquant pronouncements on the Jewish lobby in the United States:

- "The influence of American Jewry in Washington is far disproportionate to the size of the community...But so is the amount of money they contribute to [election] campaigns."[131]

    –*The Jerusalem Post*

- "On Capitol Hill, the Israel lobby commands large majorities in both the House and Senate."[132]

    –Glenn Frankel, *Washington Post Magazine*

- "I've never seen a American president – I don't care who he is – stand up to them [the Israelis]. It just boggles the mind. They always get what they want. The Israelis know what is going on all the time...If the American people understood what a grip those people have got on our government, they would rise up in arms. Our citizens certainly don't have any idea what goes on."[133]

  –Adm. Thomas Moorer, former chairman
  of the Joint Chiefs of Staff

- "Even to remark on the relative political power of the American Jewish community–whether of the Israel lobby in Washington or of Jewish influence in domestic affairs–arouses fear in some quarters of giving ammunition to the anti-Semites."[134]

  –David Biale, Noted Jewish Historian

- "But you know as well as I do that, somehow, the Israeli government is placed on a pedestal here, and to criticize it is to be immediately dubbed anti-Semitic...People are scared in this country to say wrong is wrong because the Jewish lobby is powerful – very powerful."[135]

  –Bishop Desmond Tutu, Speaking in Boston

- "A Jewish cabal has taken over the government in the United States and formed an unholy alliance with fundamentalist Christians ... There is far too much Jewish influence in the United States."[136]

  –Tam Dalyell, British MP

## *Smearing Opponents as anti-Semitic*

Two extended quotations relating to this oft-used tactic for suppressing opposition to Jewish interests are appropriate for opening this section of analysis:

> "Those charged with anti-Semitism are prey to the consequences of the distinctly human disgust, aversion and suspicion reserved for the mentally ill. Furthermore, the charge of anti-Semitism serves both as a Jewish sword and a Jewish shield. On the one hand, it is an ad hominem attack upon the character of a critic of Jewry. As such, it functions as a threat, used to intimidate and to coerce the critic or potential critic into silence, and to defame his character and dismiss his assertions if he speaks out. Thus it is an offensive weapon, a Jewish sword.
>
> Now, let us see how it functions as a defensive shield for Jewish people. The charge of anti-Semitism can provide Jews psychological insulation from negative criticism, which, even though it be legitimate, is too painful for conscious acceptance. A Jew can easily sweep the criticism from conscious awareness by saying, 'He [the critic of Jewry] is just an anti-Semite. Therefore, whatever he says about the Jews is false, and I don't have to listen to him.' In a word, it is an excellent example of the Freudian defense mechanism of rationalization.
>
> This could well be one of the major psychic forces behind this seemingly endless drive by certain Jewish organizations to 'discover anti-Semitism' in the critics of Zionism and other forms of Jewish social and political influence. The charge of anti-Semitism could thus function as a conscience-salving self-deception for Jewish people."[137]

"The accusations of anti-Semitism are getting more and more laughable with every passing day. Everyone who criticizes Israel is automatically an anti-Semite, from the simple letter-writer all the way to the president. The objective of the pro-Israeli lobby is clear: use the anti-Semitic smear to intimidate the critics of Israel and ultimately to silence them. Oftentimes, this tactic has worked, but not with those who know the stratagem.

This objective is achieved by cultivating a subtle and detestable confusion: When you criticize Israel you are criticizing the Jewish state. By criticizing the Jewish state you are criticizing the Jewish people and Judaism. Therefore, you are an anti-Semite.

It is rather distressing to see Israel and its supporters stoop that low. They cannot present their case based on its own merit...the Lobby in its true light: a pressure group that places the interest of a foreign country above that of the United States, and that plays politics at the lowest level imaginable to get what it wants."[138]

From the average American to the president of the United States, anyone courageous enough to question Jewish power and influence is immediately smeared as anti-Semitic, as the following examples will illustrate:

*The Student*

- Jess Coleman – A student at Brigham Young University, Coleman has been slandered for honest inquiry into Middle East affairs. Coleman writes, "I've been called anti-Semitic...It's inaccurate, but it's a startling political reality. The debate surrounding the Israeli-Palestinian conflict has become so polarized in recent decades that it has brought reasonable conversation to a standstill. And it's time for it to stop…Republicans and Democrats alike strongly support Israel, with eighty percent and sixty-five percent, respectively, holding favorable views of the country, according to a 2012 Gallup poll. I challenge you to find any other conceivable issue where Americans on both sides of the isle are in such strong agreement. It's not hard to see how we got here. Organizations such as the American Israel Public Affairs Committee and the Emergency Committee for Israel have effectively dictated the conversation surrounding Israel, as extremely well-funded groups with no serious competitors…I am not an anti-Semite…I'm a grown-up willing to have a discussion, and I'm waiting for everyone else to catch up."[139]

## The Scholars

- John Mearsheimer (University of Chicago) and Stephen Walt (Harvard University) – Earlier, I included within these pages an extended section from the two professors' well-written essay, *The Israel Lobby and U.S. Foreign Policy*, which was published in the *London Review of Books*. Israel-apologist extraordinaire Alan Dershowitz wasted no time in calling the essay "one-sided" and its authors "liars" and "bigots."[140] The following day on MSNBC's television program 'Scarborough Country,' Dershowitz suggested the paper had been taken from various hate sites: "every paragraph virtually is copied from a neo-Nazi Web site, from a radical Islamic Web site, from David Duke's Web site."[141] In a letter published in the *London Review of Books* in May 2006, Mearsheimer and Walt denied that they had used any racist sources for their article, writing that Dershowitz had failed to offer any evidence to support his claim.[142] That the despicable Dershowitz could get away with baselessly accusing two professors from among the finest universities in the entire country of academic fraud and slandering them both as anti-Semitic without being sued is nearly beyond comprehension, but such is Jewish power in America.

## The Political Commentator

- Pat Buchanan – A former senior advisor to Richard Nixon, Gerald Ford, and Ronald Reagan, it is safe to say that Buchanan is an expert in the functioning of our government and has experienced, firsthand, Jewish power and influence at work. Buchanan now spends most of his time as a writer and frequent guest on television's most influential political talk shows. For having the courage to question Jewish power and influence on America's domestic and foreign policy, Buchanan was wrongly and unjustly smeared by the Anti-Defamation league: "As an author, media figure, and political commentator, Patrick Buchanan publicly espouses racist, anti-Semitic, anti-Israel and anti-immigrant views" – no reasoned response to Buchanan's opinions was given by the ADL, merely labeling Buchanan as anti-Semitic has been enough to scare most Americans away from listening to what he has to say.[143] Buchanan, however, took the moral high-ground and won a de facto victory with the following eloquent response: "They charge us with anti-Semitism... The truth is, those hurling these charges harbor a passionate attachment to a nation not our own that causes them to subordinate the interests of their own country and to act on an assumption that, somehow, what's good for Israel is good for America."[144]

## The Political Nominees

- Charles W. Freeman, Jr. – This lifelong public servant honestly and correctly stated that America's unwavering support for Israel causes anti-Americanism within the Arab world and that "Israel is driving itself toward a cliff, and it is irresponsible not to question Israeli policy and to decide what is best for the American people."[145] Unsurprisingly, the pro-Israel lobby took great pains to defeat Freeman's 2009 nomination to chair the National Intelligence Council. AIPAC, the Zionist Organization of America, and Representative Steve Israel (D-NY) lead the charge against Freeman, who eventually withdrew himself from consideration from the post and "charged that he had been the victim of a concerted campaign by...the Israel lobby" – not surprisingly, that charge fell upon deaf ears in the liberal, Jewish-controlled media.[146] Recalling his ordeal, Freeman stated, "The libels on me and their easily traceable e-mail trails show conclusively that there is a powerful lobby determined to prevent any view other than its own from being aired. The tactics of the Israel lobby plumb the depths of dishonor and indecency and include character assassination, selective misquotation, the willful distortion of the record, the fabrication of falsehoods, and an utter disregard for the truth...The aim of this lobby is control of the policy process through the exercise of a veto over the appointment of people who dispute the wisdom of its views, the substitution of political correctness for analysis, and the exclusion of any and all options for decision by Americans and our government other than those that it favors."[147]

• Chuck Hagel – In 2013, Hagel was the first individual in the storied history of the United States of America to have his nomination for secretary of defense filibustered in the Senate. Hagel's crime? Making the following honest and correct claims, none of which contained ethnic, racial, or religious slurs of any kind:

–"The political reality is that the Jewish lobby intimidates a lot of people [on Capitol Hill]."[148]

–"The [American] State Department has become adjunct to the Israeli foreign minister's office."[149]

–"Israel is on its way to becoming an apartheid state."[150]

–"I think it's really dangerous to be talking about using military force against Iran."[151]

For such honest and accurate commentary, Hagel was depicted by the Jewish lobby as the modern reincarnation of Adolf Hitler. Israel-defender Elliot Abrams literally called Hagel an anti-Semite on National Public Radio, the taxpayer-funded radio station. In this instance, Abrams' despicable move backfired. Irate listeners flooded the station with letters such as the following:

> "How dare you NPR - how dare you allow discredited neocon hack Elliott Abrams to smear and mislead about Chuck Hagel on my Public Air Waves."[152]
>
> –Larry James
> Fairfax Station, Virginia

> "Questioning Israel's actions from time to time is not anti-Semitism…I can't believe you let a guy who secretly sold weapons to our enemies [Iran-Contra Affair] smear with hearsay and innuendo a guy who earned two Purple Hearts serving this country."[153]
>
> –Donn Viviani
> Honolulu, Hawaii

> "I hope you are going to have someone on the program to refute Abrams' position on the Hagel nomination… The charge that Hagel is an anti-Semite is a serious charge.

Abrams was an architect of the Iraq War, which Hagel opposed."[154]

–Chris Carlson
Portland, Oregon

Hagel's nomination was finally confirmed by the Senate after nearly two months of the Jewish lobby humiliating the American war hero. But his authority was so damaged during the confirmation process that one wonders if having Hagel as defense secretary is no longer good for the United States.

*The President of the United States of America*

- George H.W. Bush – "As a prep-school student at Phillips Andover, George H.W. Bush rescued a Jewish boy named Bruce Gelb from the grip of a bully. (Decades later, Gelb, whose father had founded Clairol, became an important financial contributor to Bush's political campaigns). As a collegian at Yale, Bush voted for Jews to be allowed into the exclusive Skull and Bones Society. As vice president of the United States, Bush coordinated America's role in the exodus of Falasha Jews from Ethiopia. And as president, Bush had his administration work for Jewish interests on several fronts – as when it helped facilitate the emigration to Israel of hundreds of thousands of Russian Jews; played a crucial role in the rescue of a second wave of Falashas; and strong-armed the United Nations into rescinding the infamous 1975 resolution that equated Zionism with racism."[155] Yet in 1991, all this was not enough to stop Israeli Minister Rehavam Ze'evi from calling Bush an "anti-Semite" when loan guarantees Israel was seeking from the United States were not being approved fast enough for the despicable Ze'evi's liking.[156]

*The Elder Statesman*

- Jimmy Carter has spent a lifetime, including his lone term as president, trying to broker peace between the Israelis and the Palestinians. In fact, the 1978 Camp David Accords mediated by Carter remain among the most influential peace agreements in world history. Yet to judge the actions of the Jewish lobby in response to the publication of Carter's 2006 book, *Palestine: Peace Not Apartheid*, one would think the former president is among the world's most ardent anti-Semites. Of course, that is exactly the feeling influential Jewish-Americans would like people to have about the former president. The fact is, Jimmy Carter does not have a hateful bone is his body. His primary goal in his twilight years has merely been to point out the suffering and terrible living conditions of the Palestinian people in both the West Bank and the Gaza Strip. But because highlighting the deplorable situation of the Palestinians paints Israel in a negative light, the dovish Carter has been subjected to the wrath of the Jewish lobby, which exceeds that of the dogs of hell. In this instance, however, mere words were not enough for Carter's Jewish attackers. A class-action lawsuit was filed by Jewish readers of Carter's book, which seeks $5 million in restitution for [wrongly] alleged distortion of facts.[157] Ironically, the Jewish lobby was further enraged when Jimmy Carter was given a 2013 award for conflict resolution by Yeshiva University, New York City's Jewish university.[158] Never at a loss for words, and rarely incapable of quickly mustering a slanderous comment with which to attack anyone with the audacity to tell the truth, Alan Dershowitz commented, "I can't imagine a worse person to honor for conflict resolution...He's never met a terrorist he didn't love, and never met an Israeli whom he did."[159] Quite a description of Carter, a man who still routinely travels to Israel to visit Jewish friends and promote peace.

## *Exploiting the Holocaust*

"The [Holocaust] is frequently exploited in America and Israel to deflect and forbid any criticism of Israel...It gives American Jews in particular a unique, retrospective 'victim identity'; it allows Israel to trump any other nation's sufferings (and justify its own excesses) with the claim that the Jewish catastrophe was unique and incomparable; and it is adduced as an all-purpose metaphor for evil – anywhere, everywhere and always – and taught to schoolchildren all over America and Europe without any reference to context or cause."[160]

–Tony Judt, *The Nation*

Indeed, it is most unconscionable that the Jewish lobby uses the Holocaust to elicit sympathy for its cause. And Jewish scholar Norman G. Finkelstein, former professor at DePaul University in Chicago, has covered this issue in his two controversial books, *The Holocaust Industry: Reflections on the Exploitation of Jewish Suffering* and *Beyond Chutzpah: On the Misuse of Anti-Semitism and the Abuse of History*, which eventually cost him his teaching position when the predictable Jewish uproar ensued.[161]

As one review of *The Holocaust Industry* notes, "It was not until the Arab-Israeli War of 1967, when Israel's evident strength brought it into line with U.S. foreign policy, that memory of the Holocaust began to acquire the exceptional prominence it enjoys today. Leaders of America's Jewish community were delighted that Israel was now deemed a major strategic asset and...exploited the Holocaust to enhance this newfound status. Their subsequent interpretations of the tragedy are often at variance with actual historical events and are employed to deflect any criticism of Israel and its supporters...Finkelstein contends that the main danger posed to the memory of Nazism's victims comes not from the distortions of Holocaust deniers but from prominent, self-proclaimed guardians of Holocaust memory. Drawing on a wealth of untapped sources...

Finkelstein concludes that the Holocaust industry has become an outright extortion racket."[162]

In 2009, the Jewish-born Gerald Kaufman, who has been a British MP since 1970, made headlines for the following assessment of the Israeli-Palestinian conflict: "My grandmother [killed by Nazi soldiers] did not die to provide cover for Israeli soldiers who are murdering Palestinian grandmothers in Gaza. The present Israeli government ruthlessly and cynically exploits the continuing guilt among Gentiles over the slaughter of Jews in the Holocaust as justification for their murder of Palestinians."[163]

In 2010, Tadeusz Pieornek, a bishop of the Roman Catholic Church, found himself in hot water when he stated, "The Holocaust only receives media coverage because of affluent Jews' financial backing, military might, and lobbying fronts, presenting a skewed version of events to the world."[164] Pieronek went on to state, "while the Holocaust was not exclusively Jewish, Jews have monopolized it in lieu of encouraging serious historical debate, free from prejudice and victimization"[165] He also alleged that "Jews today use the Holocaust as a weapon of propaganda, used to obtain benefits which are often unjustified, citing as an example the unconditional support for Israel by the U.S."[166]

In recent years, even a large segment of religious Jews has become fed up with secular Jews exploiting the Holocaust to further their Zionist ambitions. One common Hasidic Jew, speaking before cameras at a "Free Palestine" rally in London, summarized the situation as follows: "The Holocaust is now an industry for Zionists. They are using the Holocaust to commit a new Holocaust on the Palestinians. We shouldn't be exploiting the Holocaust to add to the suffering of other people. This exploitation is terrible for the Jewish people. The Zionists are killing the Jewish religion."[167]

## *Exploiting The Bible*

"Why not Kamchatka, Alaska, Mexico, or Texas? There are a great many empty countries. Why should the Jews choose a country which has a population that does not want to receive them in a particular friendly way; a small country; a country which has been neglected and derelict for centuries? It seems unusual on the part of a practical and shrewd people like the Jews to sink their effort, their sweat, and blood, their substance, into the sands, rocks, and marshes of Palestine...Well, I could, if I wished to be facetious, say it was not our responsibility – not the responsibility of the Jews who sit here – it was the responsibility of Moses, who acted from divine inspiration. He might have brought us to the United States, and instead of the Jordan might have had the Mississippi. It would have been an easier task. But he chose to stop here. We are an ancient people with old history, and you cannot deny your history and begin fresh."[168]

–Chaim Weizmann, first president of Israel

Weizmann's words, spoken in 1949, represent the common Jewish tactic of exploiting the Bible and the Jews' self-assigned role as "God's chosen people" to justify the theft of their current homeland, Palestine. As one critic writes, "this is a classic argument of Zionists and is used to gain international support and sympathy for Israel and the Zionist movement."[169] In fact, in 1937, David Ben-Gurion, Israel's first prime minister, actually told the British that the Bible is the Jewish people's mandate for living in Palestine, which is highly convenient given that Jews place no great emphasis on the Bible itself.[170]

In the new millennium, the Jewish lobby continues to exploit the Bible, especially in the United States, to gain sympathy and support for its desired goals. AIPAC, the most powerful lobbying organization in the entire world, actually devotes an entire page of its website to such exploitation. The contents of that webpage are worth noting here:

> "The biblical kingdom of David (1000 BCE), followed by Solomon, was the Jewish people's first independent nation-state, with Jerusalem as its political and spiritual capital. Over the following three millennia, the Jewish nation of Israel was conquered by numerous foreign empires including the Persians, Greeks and Romans. Mass expulsion by imperial rulers led to the majority of Jewish people being dispersed throughout the world after the destruction of the Second Temple in the year 70 CE.
>
> Despite being persecuted by these invading foreign forces, many brave Jews remained in their native Israel, continuing the Jewish inhabitance of this ancient land, without pause, until today.
>
> Those who fled under expulsion and the generations that followed never lost faith in their desire to return to the land of their forefathers and foremothers: Israel. They never lost hope of one day returning to their ancient capital of Jerusalem—a city mentioned more than 800 times in the Bible and thousands of times in more than 2,000 years of rabbinic literature.
>
> Millions of America's Christians also feel a deep and abiding connection to Israel, and demonstrate this by making religious pilgrimages, offering moral and financial support and praying for the peace of Jerusalem. Based on theology and devotion to the land that was the setting for thousands of years of biblical history, they embrace the Jewish people and their national aspirations in Israel.

Beyond faith alone, America's Christians have many reasons to support Israel: the Jewish state reflects U.S. democratic ideals, is a stable ally in a turbulent region and fervently protects all holy sites and freedom of religion for its citizens."[171]

Of course, many of America's most fanatical Evangelical Christian leaders are also complicit in this exploitation of the Bible, brainwashing their millions of mindless sheep-like followers into helping the Jewish lobby gain support for both its domestic and foreign agenda.

- "Yes, the survival of the Jewish people is a miracle of God. The return of the Jewish people to the land promised to Abraham, Isaac, and Jacob is a miracle of God. The remarkable victories of Jewish armies against overwhelming odds in successive battles in 1948, and 1967, and 1973 are clearly miracles of God. The technological marvels of Israeli industry, the military prowess, the bounty of Israeli agriculture, the fruits and flowers and abundance of the land are a testimony to God's watchful care over this new nation and the genius of this people."[172]

–Pat Robertson

–No, Mr. Robertson, the success of the Israelis over their Arab enemies in multiple wars and the prosperity of the Israeli people are works of charity carried out by the United States of America, not God. Most likely, God is wondering why the Jews refer to themselves as his "chosen people" when surely God loves all mankind equally.

- "Everything Christians do should be based upon the Biblical text…It is not possible to say, 'I am a Christian' and not love the Jewish people…We support Israel because all other nations were created by an act of man, but Israel was created by an act of God!"[173]

–The John Hagee Ministries

–No, Mr. Hagee, Israel was created in 1948 by an act of war, wherein Jews slaughtered both British and Palestinian men and women, spilling blood in the name of acquiring real estate.

Because of men like Pat Robertson and John Hagee, millions of fanatical Evangelical Christians in America believe that "the Bible predicts the future and that we are living in the last days. Their beliefs are rooted in dispensationalism, a particular way of understanding the Bible's prophetic passages, especially those in Daniel and Ezekiel in the Old Testament and the Book of Revelation in the New Testament. They make up about one-third of America's forty or fifty million Evangelical Christians and believe that the nation of Israel will play a central role in the unfolding of end-time events. In the last part of the twentieth century, dispensationalist Evangelicals became Israel's best friends—an alliance that has made a serious geopolitical difference."[174]

# CONCLUSION

Roughly seventy percent of this work has been devoted to quantifying Jewish influence in the United States of America by listing the greatest positions of power and influence in our society and showing that these same positions are largely occupied by Jews. In this manner, it is impossible to deny that Jews wield power and influence in America far beyond what their percentage of the population would dictate. Because, as we have seen, the Jewish lobby effectively contains any such talk based on anecdotal evidence or hearsay, it is necessary to quantify Jewish influence in this manner. When confronted with facts, there is less room for those who defend or dismiss Jewish power and influence in America to obfuscate.

As regards the topic of Jewish power and influence in America, half the battle is merely convincing the masses to acknowledge the monopoly that is clearly and plainly in effect – for millions of citizens are either ignorant of its existence or simply unwilling to accept it. As such, let us take one last look at the most important findings from our quantitative analysis, which are shocking given that Jews comprise just two percent of the population:

Government

- **Three of the past six chiefs of staff to the president, or fifty percent, have been Jewish**

- No less than two of the past six national security advisors, or thirty-three percent, have been Jewish
- Two of the past three senior advisors to the president, or sixty-seven percent, have been Jewish
- The vice president has his own chief of staff, of which no less than four of the past eight, or fifty percent, have been Jewish
- No less than four of the past thirteen secretaries of defense, or thirty-one percent, have been Jewish
- No less than two of the past twelve attorneys general, or seventeen percent, have been Jewish
- No less than five of the past seven secretaries of the treasury, or seventy-one percent, have been Jewish
- No less than four of the past six chairs of the Federal Reserve, or sixty-seven percent, have been Jewish
- The Securities and Exchange Commission is headed by a chairperson, of which no less than two of the past three, or sixty-seven percent, have been Jewish
- Three of the nine current Supreme Court justices, or thirty-three percent, are Jewish
- The World Bank has had just twelve presidents since its founding in 1946, of which no less than five, or forty-two percent, have been Jewish (as stated earlier, the World Bank is a non-governmental institution, yet maintains close ties to several agencies of the federal government).

Law

The most powerful and influential law groups in the United States include the following, all of which have Jewish presidents and/or directors:

- Anti-Defamation League
- American Center for Law and Justice
- American Civil Liberties Union
- Human Rights Watch

- Leadership Conference on Civil and Human Rights
- Southern Poverty Law Center

## Academia

- **No less than five of the eight Ivy League institutions, or sixty-three percent, currently have Jewish presidents**
- **No less than twenty-five of America's fifty most influential think tanks, or fifty percent, have Jewish presidents and/ or directors**
- **A recent ranking of the world's one hundred greatest living intellectuals included thirty-six Americans, of whom twenty-two, or sixty-one percent, are Jewish**

## Media

- **No less than fourteen of America's top twenty-five newspapers, or fifty-six percent, are owned, published, or edited by Jews**
- **All four of the major television broadcasting networks in the United States, or one hundred percent, have Jewish chairmen or CEOs.**
- **All three of the highest-rated cable news channels in America, or one hundred percent, have Jewish chairmen or CEOs.**

## Business

- **The 2012 Fortune 100 list shows that no less than nineteen of these one hundred elite corporations, or nineteen percent, have Jewish chairmen or CEOs.**
- **Of the top thirty hedge funds in the United States, twenty-two, or seventy-three percent, are managed by Jews.**
- **Of the top thirty private equity groups in the United States, nine, or thirty percent, are managed Jews.**

- **Of the 2012 Forbes 400 list, one hundred thirty of the four hundred richest Americans, or thirty-three percent, are Jewish.**

Entertainment

- **The "Big Six" movie studios each have a parent division and a major studio subsidiary. Nine out of twelve of these divisions and subsidiaries, or seventy-five percent, are run by Jewish-Americans.**
- **The "Big Three" recording companies control the music industry - all three, or one hundred percent, are headed by American Jews.**

Of course, the foregoing quantitative analysis is unnecessary in proving Jewish power and influence in America in light of the following quote:

> "Yes, there are many individual Jews in positions of influence in Hollywood, in network television, in sports and entertainment, and in many other areas of American public life."[175]

–Alan Dershowitz

When the foremost defender of Jewish interests known to mankind acknowledges that "there are many individual Jews in positions of influence...in American public life," one can take that to mean that Jews possess a veritable monopoly of power in the United States.

Roughly twenty percent of this work has detailed the manner in which powerful and influential Jews, without conspiring amongst one another, use their positions to support liberal and Zionist causes. In law, education, the media, entertainment, and culture,

Jewish power-players promote liberal values such as abortion, affirmative action, anarchism, anti-Americanism, anti-capitalism, and atheism. We have also witnessed the use of Jewish power in the federal government to influence both domestic and foreign policy in a manner beneficial to the state of Israel, rather than the United States.

Roughly ten percent of this work has been allotted to illustrating the suppression of opposition to Jewish influence in America, which is conducted primarily through AIPAC, the most powerful lobbying organization in the world. As we have seen, anyone courageous enough to question Jewish power and influence in America immediately finds themselves branded as anti-Semitic.

But the most telling feature of this work is that it has relied on the words of Jews themselves to press the case that, as a people, Jews are overrepresented in American society and use their power and influence for liberal and pro-Israel purposes. It is best to conclude our study in the same manner:

"As a proud Jew, I want America to know about our accomplishment. Yes, we control Hollywood ... I don't care if Americans think we are running the news media, Hollywood, Wall Street or the government. I just care that we get to keep running them."[176]
–Joel Stein, *Los Angeles Times*

"The disproportionate political power of Jews is pound for pound the greatest of any ethnic/cultural group in America...Jewish economic influence and power is disproportionately concentrated in Hollywood, television, and in the news industry"[177]
–Stephen Steinlight, American Jewish Committee

"I was much more deeply devoted to Israel than I dared to assert ... Fortified by my knowledge of Israel and my friendships there, I myself wrote most of our Middle East commentaries. As more

Arab than Jewish readers recognized, I wrote them from a pro-Israel perspective.'

—Max Frankel, former executive editor, *New York Times*

"The influence of American Jewry in Washington is far dispropor-tionate to the size of the community."

—*The Jerusalem Post*

Given that this work has relied on quantitative analysis rather than subjective opinion, and given that the vast majority of the quota-tions recounted in these pages come from the mouths of Jews, the question that presents itself is as follows: What will the Jewish lobby do to dismiss the content of books like *American Zion?* For one can-not cry "anti-Semite" against another who has merely counted the numbers of Jews in high places and used the words of Jews them-selves to show how Jewish power and influence abides in America.

Nonetheless, baseless charges of anti-Semitism are all but guaran-teed to continue as Jewish power and influence in America is fur-ther consolidated and as the use of that same power and influence is more plainly used for liberal and pro-Israel purposes in a world that is becoming more ideologically divided by the day. But there is a greater misfortune than that of an honest and well-intentioned critic of Jewish power being slandered with empty charges of anti-Semitism, and that is the silencing of the voices of the other ninety-eight percent of Americans whose opinions are equally worthy of being heard, yet are not because the mediums through which this is accomplished are at the two percent's disposal. Furthermore, and as the words of so many scholars cited is this work have de-scribed, the interests of the two percent and the interests of an entirely foreign nation are being promoted ahead of the interests of the United States of America, which is something that no loyal citizen can abide.

*"In the olden days, an anti-Semite was someone who hates Jews. These days it's someone the Jews hate. All you need to do is criticise Israel or the Israel lobby and a lot of people call you an anti-Semite."*[178]

**–Andrew Winkler, Jewish anti-Zionist**

# NOTES

[1]Shawn Ryan Rosa, *On the Precipice: Constructing a Strategic Plan to Save the American Empire from Extinction.* (Charleston, South Carolina: CreateSpace, 2013).

[2]*2010 United States Census.* U.S. Census Bureau. Retrieved 25 March 2013. <www.census.gov/2010census/data>.

[3]Arnold Dashefsky and Ira Sheskin. "Jewish Population in the United States." (University of Connecticut, 2011). The authors confirm that Jews comprise two percent of the American population.

[4]Ner LeElef. "World Jewish Population." *Judaism Online.* Retrieved 25 March 2013. <www.simpletoremember.com/vitals/world-jewish-population.htm>.

[5]*2008 Population Census.* Israeli Central Bureau of Statistics. <www.cbs.gov.il/census/census/main_mifkad08_e.html>.

[6]Lenni Brenner. "The Demographics of American Jews." *CounterPunch.* Retrieved 25 March 2013. <www.counterpunch.org/2003/10/24/the-demographics-of-american-jews>.

[7]Arnold Dashefsky and Ira Sheskin. "Jewish Population in the United States." Dashefsky and Sheskin are the source of all figures regarding America's Jewish population cited in this section.

[8]Ibid.

[9]Ibid.

[10]Ibid.

[11]"U.S. Religious Landscape Survey, 2008." The Pew Forum on Religion & Public Life. Retrieved 25 March 2013. <www.pewforum.org>. All demographic statistics concerning Jews, Evangelical Protestants, Mainline Protestants, and Catholics have been derived from this report.

[12]Ibid.

[13]Ibid.

[14]Ibid.

[15]Ibid.

[16]Ibid.

[17]Ibid.

[18]Ibid.

[19]"Office of Management and Budget." *Wikipedia Online Encyclopedia.* Retrieved 25 March 2013. <www.en.wikipedia.org/wiki/Office_of_Management_and_Budget>.

[20]United States Department of Defense. Retrieved 25 March 2013. <www.defense.gov/about>.

[21]"United States Department of Defense." *Wikipedia Online Encyclopedia.* Retrieved 25 March 2013. <www.en.wikipedia.org/wiki/United_States_Department_of_Defense>.

[22]Ibid.

[23]Our Government - "The Executive Branch." Retrieved 25 March 2013. <www.whitehouse.gov/our-government/executive-branch>.

[24]Ibid.

[25]Ibid.

[26]"United States Department of Justice." *Wikipedia Online Encyclopedia.* Retrieved 25 March 2013. <www.en.wikipedia.org/wiki/United_States_Department_of_Justice>.

[27]Our Government – "The Executive Branch."

[28]"United States Department of the Treasury." *Wikipedia Online Encyclopedia.* Retrieved 25 March 2013. <www.en.wikipedia.org/wiki/United_States_Department_of_the_Treasury>.

[29]"United States Securities and Exchange Commission." *Wikipedia Online Encyclopedia.* Retrieved 24 March 2013. <www.en.wikipedia.org/wiki/U.S._Securities_and_Exchange_Commission>.

[30]Arnold Dashefsky and Ira Sheskin. "Jewish Population in the United States."

[31]Ibid.

[32]*2010 United States Census.* U.S. Census Bureau.

[33]Ibid.

[34]American Center for Law and Justice. Retrieved 24 March 2013. <www.aclj.org/our-mission>.

[35]American Civil Liberties Union. Retrieved 24 March 2013. <www.aclu.org/about-aclu-0>.

[36]Anti-Defamation League. Retrieved 24 March 2013. <www.adl.org/about-adl>.

[37]Human Rights Watch. Retrieved 24 March 2013. <www.hrw.org/about>.

[38]Leadership Council on Civil and Human Rights. Retrieved 24 March 2013. <www.civilrights.org/about>.

[39]Southern Poverty Law Center. Retrieved 24 March 2013. <www.splcenter.org/what-we-do>.

[40]William F. Buckley, Jr., *God & Man At Yale* (Washington: Regnery Publishing, 2002). Buckley's is the seminal work on liberalism within the academic world.

[41]James G. McGann. "2011 Global Go To Think Tanks Index Report." (University of Pennsylvania, 2011).

[42]"The Prospect/Foreign Press Top 100 Public Intellectuals." *InfoPlease*. Retrieved 23 March 2013. <www.infoplease.com/spot/topintellectuals.html>.

[43]Meg Sullivan. "Media Bias is Real, Finds UCLA Political Scientist." *UCLA Newsroom*. Retrieved 24 March 2013. <www.newsroom.ucla.edu/portal/ucla/Media-Bias-Is-Real-Finds-UCLA-6664.aspx?RelNum=6664>.

[44]Neal Lulofs. "The Top U.S. Newspapers for September 2012." *WordPress*. Retrieved 23 March 2013. <www.accessabc.wordpress.com/2012/10/30/the-top-u-s-newspapers-for-september-2012>.

[45]"List of Syndicated Columnists." *Wikipedia Online Encyclopedia*. Retrieved 11 March 2013. <www.en.wikipedia.org/wiki/list_of_syndicated_columnists>.

[46]"Fox News Channel Marks Decade as the Number One Cable News Network." *Fox News*. Retrieved 23 March 2013. <www.press.foxnews.com/2012/01/fox-news-channel-marks-decade-as-the-number-one-cable-news-network>.

[47]"*Fortune* 500." *CNNMoney*. Retrieved 1 April 2013. <www.money.cnn.com/magazines/fortune/fortune500/2012/full_list>.

[48]"List of Hedge Funds." *Wikipedia Online Encyclopedia*. Retrieved 1 April 2013. <www.en.wikipedia.org/wiki/List_of_hedge_funds>.

[49]"List of Private Equity Firms." *Wikipedia Online Encyclopedia*. Retrieved 1 April 2013. <www.en.wikipedia.org/wiki/List_of_private_equity_firms>.

[50]"*Forbes* 400." *Forbes*. Retrieved 28 March 2013. <www.forbes.com/forbes-400/list>.

[51]Ibid.

[52]"List of Public REITs in the United States." Wikipedia Online Encyclopedia. Retrieved 28 March 2013. <www.en.wikipedia.org/wiki/List_of_public_REITs_in_the_United_States>.

[53]"Top 10 Largest Home Builders in the United States." *The Real Estate Bloggers*. Retrieved 28 March 2013. <www.therealestatebloggers.com/top-10-largest-home-builders-in-united-states>.

[54]"Major Film Studio." *Wikipedia Online Encyclopedia*. Retrieved 30 March 2013. <www.en.wikipedia.org/wiki/Major_film_studio#Current_majors>.

[55]"The 3 Major Record Labels Left Standing." *MusicClout*. Retrieved 30 March 2013. <www.musicclout.hubpages.com/hub/The-3-Major-Record-Labels-Left-Standing>.

[56]"How to Make It in the Art World – Know These 100 People." *New York Magazine*. Retrieved 23 March 2013. <www.nymag.com/arts/art/rules/insiders-2012-4>.

[57]*Arts Participation 2008: Highlights from a National Survey*. National Endowment for the Arts. Retrieved 2 April 2013. <www.arts.gov/publications/arts-participation-2008-highlights-national-survey-0>

[58]New York City Department of Cultural Affairs. Retrieved 28 March 2013. <www.nyc.gov/html/dcla/html/about/message.shtml>.

[59]"Big Five (Orchestras)." *Wikipedia Online Encyclopedia*. Retrieved 28 March 2013. <www.en.wikipedia.org/wiki/Big_Five_(orchestras)>.

[60]"Broadway Theatre." *Wikipedia Online Encyclopedia*. Retrieved 28 March 2013. <www.en.wikipedia.org/wiki/Broadway_theatre>.

[61]Ibid.

[62]"12 Facts on the Fashion Industry in the United States." *Business Vibes*. Retrieved 1 April 2013. <www.businessvibes.com/blog/12-facts-fashion-industry-united-states>.

[63]"The U.S. Wine Market: Facts & Figures." *Vins de Provence*. Retrieved 23 March 2013. <www.res.franceguide.com/us/press_2012/weblinks/vin_de_provence_facts_figures.pdf>.

[64]Michael Cervin. "Top 100 Most Influential People in the U.S. Wine Industry." *IntoWine*. Retrieved 23 March 2013. <www.intowine.com/intowinecom-annual-%E2%80%9Ctop-100-most-influential-people-us-wine-industry-%E2%80%93-2012-part-i>.

[65]Cellar Tracker. Retrieved 24 March 2013. <www.cellartracker.com/about.asp>.

[66]Full Circle Wine Solutions. Retrieved 24 March 2013. <www.winecouch.com/index.php/page/show/43>.

[67]"The U.S. Professional Sports Market & Franchise Value Report , 2011." W.R. Hambrecht & Co. Sports Finance Group. Retrieved 25 March 2013. <www.s3.amazonaws.com/zanran_storage/wrhambrecht.com/ContentPages/2439776862.pdf>.

[68]"Election Reference Information: Jewish Voting Record (1916-2012)." *Jewish Virtual Library*. Retrieved 25 March 2013. <www.jewishvirtuallibrary.org/jsource/US-Israel/jewvote/html>.

[69]Ibid.

[70]Ibid.

[71]"Southern Poverty Law Center." Wikipedia Online Encyclopedia. Retrieved 28 March 2013. <www.en.wikipedia.org/wiki/Southern_Poverty_Law_Center>.

[72]"Anti-Defamation League." *Wikipedia Online Encyclopedia*. Retrieved 28 March 2013. <www.en.wikipedia.org/wiki/Anti-Defamation_League>.

[73]"Human Rights Watch." *Wikipedia Online Encyclopedia*. Retrieved 28 March 2013. <www.en.wikipedia.org/wiki/Human_Rights_Watch>.

[74]Kevin MacDonald. "Liberal Bias In Academia: The Role of Jewish Academics in the Creation and Maintenance of Academic Liberalism." Retrieved 9 April 2013. <www.educate-yourself.org/en/liberalbiasacademia10aug12.shtml>.

[75]Emily Esfahani Smith. "Survey shocker: Liberal profs admit they'd discriminate against conservatives in hiring, advancement." *The Washington Times*. Retrieved 9 April 2013. <www.washingtontimes.com/news/2012/aug/1/liberal-majority-on-campus-yes-were-biased>.

[76]Ibid.

[77]"David Horowitz's List of 100 Most Dangerous Professors in U.S." *Inter-Activist Info Exchange*. Retrieved 11 April 2013. <www.interactivist.autonomedia.org/node/5041>.

[78]"Media Bias in the United States." *Wikipedia Online Encyclopedia*. Retrieved 11 April 2013. <www.en.wikipedia.org/wiki/Media_bias_in_the_United_States>.

[79]Caleb Galoozis. "Media Basis, Alive and Well." *Harvard University Institute of Politics*. Retrieved 11 April 2013. <www.iop.harvard.edu/media-bias-alive-and-well>.

[80]S. Robert Lichter, Stanley Rothman, and Linda Lichter, *The Media Elite: America's New Power-Brokers*. (Bethesda, Maryland: Adler & Adler, 1986).

[81]"Media Bias – Who Do We Believe?" *The Los Angeles Post*. Retrieved 11 April 2013. <www.thelosangelespost.org/media-bias-believe>.

[82]Warner Todd Huston. "Top 10 Most Left-Biased American Journalists." *Publius' Forum*. Retrieved 11 April 2013. <www.publiusforum.com/2010/07/23/top-ten-most-left-biased-american-journalists>.

[83]Ibid.

[84]Ibid.

[85]Ibid.

[86]Ibid.

[87]Ibid.

[88]Ben Shapiro, *Primetime Propaganda: The True Hollywood Story of How the Left Took Over Your TV.* (New York, Broadside Books, 2012).

[89]Lindsay Powers. "Hollywood Accused of Rampant Liberal Bias in New Book." *The Hollywood Reporter.* Retrieved 11 April 2013. <www.hollywoodreporter. com/news/hollywood-accused-rampant-liberal-bias-193304>.

[90]Ibid.

[91]Ibid.

[92]Ibid.

[93]Ibid.

[94]Ibid.

[95]Ibid.

[96]"Top 10 Most Obnoxious Hollywood Liberals." *Human Events.* Retrieved 11 April 2013. <www.humanevents.com/2011/05/14/top-10-most-obnoxious-hollywood-liberals>.

[97]"Profiles in Liberal Ignorance, Hate, and Intolerance: Larry David." *Vocal Minority.* Retrieved 11 April 2013. <www.vocalminority.typad.com/blog/2009/10/prof.html>.

[98]"Harrison Ford." *Wikipedia Online Encyclopedia.* Retrieved 11 April 2013. <www.en.wikipedia.org/wiki/Harrison_Ford>.

[99]Stephen Silverman. "Actress Sparks Furor over 9/11 Remarks." *People.* Retrieved 11 April 2013. <www.people.com/people/article/0,,1054440,00. html>.

[100]"Liberal Celebrities." *UPI.* Retrieved 11 April 2013. <www.upi.com/News_Photos/Entertainment/Liberal-Celebrities/fp/6010>.

[101]"Top 10 Most Obnoxious Hollywood Liberals." *Human Events.*

[102]"Liberal Celebrities." *UPI.*

[103]Ibid.

[104]Ibid.

[105]Ibid.

[106]"Top 10 Most Obnoxious Hollywood Liberals." *Human Events.*

[107]Skip Stone. "Hippies from A to Z." *HipPlanet.* Retrieved 13 April 2013. <www.hipplanet.com/books/atoz/friends.htm>.

[108]"Peter Coyote." *Wikipedia Online Encyclopedia.* Retrieved 13 April 2013. <www.en.wikipedia.org/wiki/Peter_Coyote>.

[109]"Bernardine Dohrn." *Wikipedia Online Encyclopedia.* Retrieved 13 April 2013. <www.en.wikipedia.org/wiki/Bernardine_Dohrn>.

[110]Skip Stone. "Hippies from A to Z."

[111]Ibid.

[112]Ibid.

[113]"William Kunstler." *Wikipedia Online Encyclopedia.* Retrieved 13 April 2013. <www.en.wikipedia.org/wiki/William_Kunstler>.

[114]Skip Stone. "Hippies from A to Z."

[115]"Bill Maher." *Wikipedia Online Encyclopedia.* Retrieved 13 April 2013. <www.en.wikipedia.org/wiki/Bill_Maher>.

[116]Philip Dhingra. "Who is in Bernard Goldberg's 100 People Who Are Screwing Up America? And Why?" Retrieved 13 April 2013. <www.philosophistry.com/specials/100-people.html>.

[117]Ibid.

[118]Ibid.

[119]"The Daily Show." *Wikipedia Online Encyclopedia.* Retrieved 13 April 2013. <www.en.wikipedia.org/wiki/The_Daily_Show>.

[120]"Barbara Walters: The Closeted Liberal." *WordPress* Retrieved 13 April 2013. <www.inrareform.wordpress.com/2007/05/03/barbara-walters-the-closeted-liberal>.

[121]"Summary of U.S. Foreign Aid from 2001-2006." *Vaughn's Summaries: General Knowledge Reference.* Retrieved 9 July 2011. <www.vaughns-1-pagers.com/politics/us-foreign-aid.htm>. All data provided in this report has been taken from the U.S. Department of State and the U.S. Agency for International Development.

[122]Ibid.

[123]Jimmy Carter, *Palestine: Peace Not Apartheid* (New York: Simon & Schuster, 2006); "Summary of U.S. Foreign Aid: 2001-2006." *Vaughn's Summaries: General Knowledge Reference.*

[124]"Islam." *Encyclopedia Britannica Online.* Retrieved 10 July 2011. <www.britannica.com/EBchecked/topic/295507/Islam>. The world's Muslim population is estimated to be between 1.1 – 1.2 billion.

[125]John Mearsheimer and Stephen Walt. "The Israel Lobby." *London Review of Books.* Retrieved 13 April 2013. <www.lrb.co.uk./v28/n06/john-mearsheimer/the-israel-lobby>.

[126]Ibid.

[127]J.J. Goldberg. "Jewish Power: Inside the American Jewish Establishment." *The Washington Post.* Retrieved 13 April 2013. <www.

washingtonpost.com/wp-srv/style/longterm/books/chap1/jewish-power.htm>; Paul Findley, *They Dare to Speak Out: People and Institutions Confront Israel's Lobby.* (Westport, Connecticut: Lawrence Hill Books, 1985).

[128]Ibid.

[129]Ibid.

[130]David Postman. "An Interview with former President Jimmy Carter." *Seattle Times.* Retrieved 13 April 2013. <www.seattletimes.com/html/localnews/2003475989_webcarterqanda13.html>.

[131]Mark Weber. "A Straight Look at the Jewish Lobby." *Institute for Historical Review.* Retrieved 23 March 13. <www.ihr.org/leaflets/jewishlobby.shtml>.

[132]Glenn Frankel. "A Beautiful Friendship." *The Washington Post.* Retrieved 13 April 2013. <www.washingtonpost.com/wp-dyn/content/article/2006/07/12/AR2006071201627.html>.

[133]Mark Weber. "A Straight Look at the Jewish Lobby."

[134]J.J. Goldberg. "Jewish Power: Inside the American Jewish Establishment."

[135]Mark Weber. "A Straight Look at the Jewish Lobby."

[136]Ibid.

[137]Paul Grubach. "A Critique of the Charge of Anti-Semitism: The moral and political legitimacy of criticizing Jewry." *Institute for Historical Review.* Retrieved 15 April 2013. <www.ihr.org/jhr/v08/v08p185_Grubach.html>.

[138]Unattributed. Retrieved 15 April 2013. <www.users.cloud9.net/~recross/israel-watch/Issues/antiSemitism.html>.

[139]Jess Coleman. "I Am Not an Anti-Semite." *The Huffington Post.* Retrieved 15 April 2013. <www.huffingtonpost.com/jess-coleman/israel-support_b_2879376.html>.

[140]"Alan Dershowitz." Wikipedia Online Encyclopedia. Retrieved 15 April 2013. <www.en.wikipedia.org/wiki/Alan_Dershowitz>.

[141]Ibid.

[142]Ibid.

[143]"Pat Buchanan: In His Own Words." *Anti-Defamation League.* Retrieved 15 April 2013. <www.archive.adl.org/special_reports/buchanan_own_words/buchanan_intro.asp>.

[144]Ibid.

[145]Helene Cooper and Mark Mazzetti. "Israel Stance Was Undoing of Nominee for Intelligence Post." *New York Times.* Retrieved 15 April 2013. <www.nytimes.com/2009/03/12/washington/12lobby.html?_r=0>.

[146]"Charles W. Freeman, Jr." Wikipedia Online Encyclopedia. Retrieved 15 April 2013. <www.en.wikipedia.org/wiki/Charles_W._Freeman,_Jr.>.

[147]Ibid.

[148]"ECI Ad on Chuck Hagel in Hill and WSJ." *The Weekly Standard.* Retrieved 15 April 2013. <www.weeklystandard.com/blogs/eci-ad-chuck-hagel-hill-and-wsj_703220.html>.

[149]Ibid.

[150]Ibid.

[151]Ibid.

[152]Edward Schumacher-Matos. "Allowing Hagel to be Called 'Anti-Semitic' on NPR." *National Public Radio.* Retrieved 15 April 2013. <www.npr.org/blogs/ombudsman/2013/01/27/170398305/allowing-hagel-to-be-called-anti-semitic-on-npr>.

[153]Ibid.

[154]Ibid.

[155]Jason Maoz. "Back to the Future: A Political Excursion." *The Jewish Press.* Retrieved 15 April 2013. <www.jewishpress.com/indepth/front-page/back-to-the-future-a-political-excursion/2012/10/24/0/?print>.

[156]"Rehavam Ze'evi." *Wikipedia Online Encyclopedia.* Retrieved 15 April 2013. <www.en.wikipedia.org/wiki/Rehavam_Ze'evi#Controversy>.

[157]Jim Galloway. "A $5 million lawsuit against Jimmy Carter for the 'fiction' of his Middle East book." *Political Insider.* Retrieved 15 April 2013. <www.blogs.ajc.com/political-insider-jim-galloway/2011/02/02/a-5-million-lawsuit-against-jimmy-carter-for-the-fiction-of-his-middle-east-book>.

[158]Martha T. Moore. "Award for Jimmy Carter fuels outcry at Jewish university." *USA Today.* Retrieved 15 April 2013. <www.usatoday.com/story/news/politics/2013/04/10/jimmy-carter-cardozo-law-award>.

[159]Ibid.

[160]Mark Weber. "Holocaust Remembrance: What's Behind the Campaign?" *Institute for Historical Review.* Retrieved 15 April 2013. <www.ihr.org/leaflets/holocaust_remembrance.shtml>.

[161]Norman G. Finkelstein, *The Holocaust Industry.* (London: Verso Books, 2000); Norman G. Finkelstein, *Beyond Chutzpah: On the Misuse of Anti-Semitism and the Abuse of History.* (University of California Press, 2005); "U.S. prof who says Jews abuse Holocaust to curb critics resigns." *Asso-*

*ciated Press.* Retrieved 15 April 2013. <www.haaretz.com/news/u-s-prof-who-says-jews-abuse-holocaust-to-curb-critics-resigns-1.228982>.

[162]Unattributed. *Amazon.* Retrieved 15 April 2013. <www.amazon.com/The-Holocaust-Industry-Reflections-Exploitation/dp/185984488X>.

[163]Rabbi Rafi Rank. "Exploiting the Holocaust." *Jewish Post.* Retrieved 15 April 2013. <www.jewishpost.com/cyber_rav/exploiting-the-holocaust.html>.

[164]"Jews Exploit Holocaust." *The Jerusalem Post.* Retrieved 15 April 2013. <www.jpost.com/Jewish-World/Jewish-News/Jews-exploit-Holocaust>.

[165]Ibid.

[166]Ibid.

[167]Unattributed. "Religious Jews Explain How Zionist Jews Exploit the Holocaust." *YouTube.* Retrieved 15 April 2013. <www.youtube.com/watch?v=wiFj6q1410k>.

[168]"Chaim Weizmann: A Brief Biography & Quotes." *Palestine Remembered.* Retrieved 15 April 2013. <www.palestineremembered.com/Acre/Famous-Zionist-Quotes/Story645.html>.

[169]"Bible & Holocaust Exploitation." *Palestine Remembered.* Retrieved 15 April 2013. <www.palestineremembered.com/Acre/Famous-Zionist-Quotes/Story706.html>.

[170]Ibid.

[171]"Biblical Heritage." *American Israel Public Affairs Committee.* Retrieved 15 April 2013. <www.aipac.org/why-israel-matters/biblical-heritage>.

[172]Pat Robertson. "Why Evangelical Christians Support Israel." Retrieved 15 April 2013. <www.patrobertson.com/speeches/israellauder.asp>.

[173]John Hagee. "Why Christians Should Support Israel." Retrieved 15 April 2013. <www.jhm.org/home/about/whysupportisrael>.

[174]Timothy P. Weber. "On the Road to Armageddon: How evangelicals became Israel's best friend." *BeliefNet.* Retrieved 15 April 2013. <www.beliefnet.com/faiths/christians/end-times/on-the-road-to-armageddon.aspx>.

[175]Alan Dershowitz. "Do Jews Control the Media?" *Huffington Post.* Retrieved 15 April 2013. <www.huffingtonpost.com/alan-dershowitz/do-jews-control-the-media_b_753227.html>.

[176]Mark Weber. "A Straight Look at the Jewish Lobby."

[177]Ibid.

[178]Robert Lindsay and Andrew Winkler. "Elie Wiesel and the Big Lie." Retrieved 15 April 2013. <www.whale.to/b/lindsay.html>.